CULTURES OF THE WORLD

MOROCCO

Pat Seward

MARSHALL CAVENDISH
New York • London • Sydney

Reference edition published 1995 by
Marshall Cavendish Corporation
2415 Jerusalem Avenue
P.O. Box 587
North Bellmore
New York 11710

© Times Editions Pte Ltd 1995

Originated and designed by
Times Books International, an imprint of
Times Editions Pte Ltd

Printed in Singapore

Library of Congress Cataloging-in-Publication Data:
Seward, Pat.
   Morocco / Pat Seward.
     p. cm.—(Cultures Of The World)
   Includes bibliographical references (p.) and index.
   ISBN 0-7614-0170-9 (Morocco)
   ISBN 0-7614-0167-9 (Set)
   1. Morocco—Juvenile literature. [1. Morocco] I. Title.
II. Series.
DT305.S49 1995
964—dc20   94–43343
            CIP
            AC

Cultures of the World

Editorial Director	Shirley Hew
Managing Editor	Shova Loh
Editors	Elizabeth Berg
	Dinah Lee
	Azra Moiz
	Sue Sismondo
Picture Editor	Susan Jane Manuel
Production	Anthoney Chua
Design	Tuck Loong
	Felicia Wong
	Loo Chuan Ming
	Wendy Koh
Illustrators	Chow Kok Keong
	Anuar bin Abdul Rahim
MCC Editorial Director	Evelyn M. Fazio

INTRODUCTION

Morocco is a land of geographic contrasts—landscapes of lush beauty and stark drama—and many social contradictions. It is a country with a long history and a sophisticated culture, yet it only became independent in our modern sense in 1956. It is, therefore, a young nation. For centuries it was isolated from the mainstream of world events, but in the last 20 years it has begun to play a significant role in European, African, and Arab affairs.

In many ways Morocco, at least in the north and the big cities, has a European and especially a French feel about it. But this is only a facade behind which centuries-old traditions still flourish. It is an Arab nation on the African continent with close economic and historic ties to Europe. There are many tensions between rich and poor, traditionalist and modernist, and yet outsiders recognize the presence of a moderate force in an area of the world that is presently volatile and unpredictable.

CONTENTS

A Moroccan artisan carefully paints a piece of furniture.

CONTENTS

A seminomad cooking in her tent.

GEOGRAPHY

MOROCCO IS UNIQUE in many ways, not the least of which is its position as the African country closest to Europe. The Mediterranean Sea is Morocco's northern border, with the port city of Tangier facing the southernmost point of Spain just across the Strait of Gibraltar.

The country's western border is the Atlantic Ocean, while a large part of its eastern limit is a land border with Algeria. On this side, but farther south and west, Morocco's border is in dispute following Spain's withdrawal from its former colony of Rio d'Oro in the 1970s. This land—now generally known as the Western Sahara—is claimed by Morocco. Legally therefore, Morocco covers 177,117 square miles (458,730 sq km)—about the size of Washington and Oregon states combined. If the Western Sahara is included, it covers 274,461 square miles (710,850 sq km).

Morocco divides up into five major areas: the Mediterranean coast; the Atlantic coast; the lowlands and plains, where most of the major cities are located; the Rif and Atlas mountain ranges; and finally, the pre-Sahara.

In ancient myth the Rock of Gibraltar and Jebel Musa (in Ceuta on the most northerly point of Morocco) were known as the Pillars of Hercules. The story goes that they were formed when Hercules, one of the most celebrated heroes of classical mythology, tore a mountain apart in order to get to Gades, modern Cádiz, on Spain's southwestern coast.

Opposite: **There are scarcely any easy routes across the High Atlas, but the numerous mountain tracks are well used by the local population living in the mountain valleys, often in compact fortified villages.**

Left: **Melilla is a Spanish enclave surrounded by Moroccan land.**

Various stories attempt to explain how the Atlas mountains got their name. Perhaps the most plausible myth is that of Atlas, who supported the pillars separating heaven and earth. The Greeks believed these pillars rested in the sea somewhere beyond their western horizon. Over the passage of many centuries, the name Atlas was transferred to the peaks of the westernmost mountains of North Africa, which were seen as supporting the sky above.

AFRICAN MOUNTAINS AND SPANISH ENCLAVES

In the north the Rif Mountains run along the Mediterranean coast, rising steeply from the sea to heights of more than 6,000 feet (1,828 m). Farther south are three separate mountain chains that cross the country diagonally. They divide the fertile coastal plains from the Sahara Desert.

The most northerly of the three is the Middle Atlas, which overlooks the plain south of the foothills of the Rif. A narrow gap in this range makes possible the only reasonably easy land route between western Algeria and the Atlantic Ocean. Much of the range consists of a limestone plateau dissected by river gorges and punctuated by volcanic craters. It is also flanked by two rivers, the Sebou flowing into the Atlantic and the Moulouya into the Mediterranean.

To the south the Middle Atlas merges into the High Atlas—the central, most formidable, and highest of the three ranges. Many a peak here rises to 12,000 feet (3,657 m), and snow-clad summits are seen in the winter.

The most southerly range, the Anti-Atlas, is the shortest, lowest, and most sparsely populated of the three. Its barren southern slopes are slashed by many gorges but softened by the green of cultivated palm groves. Beyond are the endless wastes of the Sahara sands.

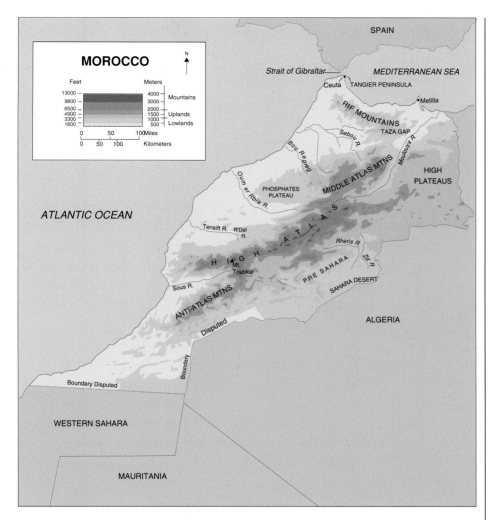

MOROCCO

Feet | Meters
13000 | 4000 — Mountains
9800 | 3000
6500 | 2000
4900 | 1500 — Uplands
3300 | 1000
1600 | 500 — Lowlands

0 50 100 Miles
0 50 100 Kilometers

N

ATLANTIC OCEAN

SPAIN

Strait of Gibraltar

MEDITERRANEAN SEA

Ceuta   TANGIER PENINSULA

Melilla

RIF MOUNTAINS

Sebou R.

TAZA GAP

Bou Regreg

Oum er Rbia R.

PHOSPHATES PLATEAU

MIDDLE ATLAS MTNS

Moulouya R.

HIGH PLATEAUS

Tensift R.   R'Dat R.

H I G H   A T L A S

Mt. Toubkal

Rheris R.

Ziz R.

PRE SAHARA

SAHARA DESERT

Sous R.

ANTI-ATLAS MTNS.

Disputed

ALGERIA

Boundary

Boundary Disputed

WESTERN SAHARA

MAURITANIA

Mt Toubkal, at 13,670 feet (4,101 m), is both Morocco's highest mountain and the highest peak in North Africa.

CEUTA AND MELILLA

In the 1970s Spain relinquished its claims to its Rio d'Oro colony south of Morocco. However, it still retains two enclaves—tiny patches of Spanish soil surrounded by Moroccan territory—at Ceuta on the Mediterranean coast close to Tangier and at Melilla near the Algerian border. These are accidents of history in the same way that Britain still retains Gibraltar on Spain's southern coast.

Both enclaves have long histories going back to Phoenician and Roman times. Today they are something of an embarrassment, particularly to Spain. The Spanish legislature is currently considering granting autonomous status to these two enclaves.

COASTS

Morocco is bounded by the sea on two sides. The Mediterranean coast is, by and large, a mixture of sandy and more rugged beaches backed by cliffs and sandwiched between rocky inlets and headlands. Bathing is relatively safe, and the scenery is often dramatic. For these reasons, the area is becoming increasingly popular with tourists. Tourism is one of the country's fastest-growing industries and is important for the jobs it creates and the much-needed foreign exchange it generates.

The Atlantic coast near Tan-Tan.

Morocco's Mediterranean coast is still generally unspoiled. Tétouan at the western end is a beautiful town with a long history. Several small resorts are nearby. Al Hoceima, halfway along the coast, is the area's main resort. Oudja, one of Morocco's largest cities, is on the Algerian border at the eastern end of the coastal region.

By contrast with the Mediterranean, vast stretches of sandy beach washed by long Atlantic waves characterize the country's west coast. As on the northern coast, there are many lively seaside towns and a few major vacation resorts. In particular, Agadir in the south is fast becoming a winter playground for sun-starved northern Europeans. In addition to new resorts, there are several ancient cities, such as Asilah, Al-Jadida, and Essaouira.

Morocco has around 21 ports of some importance. Of its nine international ports, seven—Tangier, Kénitra, Mohammedia, Casablanca, Safi, Agadir, and El Aaiún—are situated along the Atlantic coast.

The Middle Atlas Mountains are home to seminomadic communities that spend the winter months in the valleys but move to the higher slopes in summer to find pasture for their sheep and goats.

COASTAL PLAINS AND HINTERLAND

Stretching inland from the coast is an extensive area of lowland enclosed to the north by the Rif Mountains and to the east and south by the Middle and High Atlas ranges. These coastal and inland plains are Morocco's most densely populated areas. The country's major cities—Casablanca, the commercial capital, Rabat, the political capital, Marrakech, and Fès—are located either on the Atlantic coast or in the fertile lowland plains.

Across the barrier of the Atlas mountains, to the east and south, Morocco is a land of arid, rolling plateaus and, especially in the northeast, of rocky tablelands, towering ravines, and fortified villages set in green oases. Towns here are situated on the edge of the Sahara. Er Rachidia is a bustling and prosperous market; Erfoud is the last major stop before the sand dunes begin at Merzouga. Ouarzazate and the surrounding areas rose to fame as locations for various desert film epics. Farther west is the walled city of Taroudant. Beyond these isolated oases of civilization lie the vast expanses of the Sahara. In this great emptiness, nevertheless, there are treasures—valuable minerals such as phosphates and possibly oil—that fuel the ongoing disputes over the Western Sahara.

Morocco has a coastline that extends for 2,180 miles (3,488 km), and Moroccan waters contain some of the world's richest fisheries.

THE VAGARIES OF SUN AND RAIN

Morocco has been described as "a cold country with a hot sun." In fact its climate, although undeniably hot in summer, is extremely varied, and some regions can be quite cold.

Moroccans living near the north coast enjoy Mediterranean conditions. Farther south there is both greater heat and greater humidity in semitropical areas. Inland, people have to cope with greater extremes and more sudden variations in temperature, whereas to the south and east the pre-Sahara and the desert proper are subject to desert conditions—unremitting high temperatures by day and biting cold at night.

The upper elevations of the High Atlas range are under snow from November through April.

The lands north and west of the Atlas Mountains, including the Rif Mountains, are subject to cool, wet winters and dry, moderately hot summers. Conditions everywhere vary according to latitude and altitude as well as proximity to the Atlantic coast where sea breezes lessen the summer heat. Southerly coastal areas can be humid but also intensely hot if, as occasionally happens, dry winds blow up from the Sahara and dry out the lowlands.

Mountain dwellers endure hard, cold winters with heavy snowfall in the highest parts and pleasantly hot summers. Lowlands away from the coasts tend to be intolerably hot and stifling in summer and unpleasantly cold and damp in winter. In the rest of the country the climate becomes progressively more arid and extreme the farther east and south one goes.

The dunes of Tinfou in the Sahara Desert.

Drought is one of Morocco's main problems. If there was more rain and more reliable rain, the country's agricultural potential could be better exploited. In the 1980s and 90s, insufficient rain severely affected agricultural production on otherwise fertile land and caused many economic and social problems.

NOT ENOUGH WATER

In the Rif Mountains and northern parts of the Middle Atlas, rainfall averages more than 29 inches (74 cm) per year. In other parts of the Middle Atlas, in the High Atlas, and in the northern half of the Atlantic lowlands, average rainfall is between 15 and 29 inches (38–74 cm) per year. Farther south, in the southern lowlands and the Anti-Atlas, rain becomes scarcer—between eight and 15 inches (20–38 cm)—and also more variable, insufficient for the cultivation of grain crops without irrigation. East and south of the Atlas Mountains, rainfall is even scarcer and more unpredictable. The Sahara areas might receive four inches (10 cm) of rain.

SELECTED AVERAGE TEMPERATURES (MAXIMUM AND MINIMUM):

Ouarzazate (in the pre-Sahara):
Summer 104°F (39°C)
Winter 34°F (1°C)

Ketama (in the Rif Mountains):
Summer 80°F (26°C)
Winter 30°F (-1°C)

Tangier (on the Mediterranean coast):
Summer 80°F (26°C)
Winter 46°F (8°C)

Casablanca (on the Atlantic coast):
Summer 78°F (25°C)
Winter 44°F (6°)

ANCIENT ANIMALS

Ancient rock carvings in the south and mosaics dating from the first two centuries A.D. at the Roman city of Volubilis in the north reveal a countryside and a climate somewhat different from those of today. The land around Volubilis is some of the most fertile in North Africa. It supplied the Roman Empire with wheat and olive oil, as well as lions and other wild beasts for the infamous Roman "games." In addition to lions, there were bears and elephants and, farther south, ostriches and antelope—animals only seen today in the protected surroundings of wildlife parks.

Roman thirst for bloodshed as entertainment, a deteriorating climate, and prolonged and relentless hunting in more modern times have combined to deprive Morocco of many species of animals. A few lions survived in the Middle Atlas ranges until the 1920s, but the elephants that once were said to infest the area around Rabat on the Atlantic coast are gone forever. So too are the ostrich, the bubal hartebeest, and several other large mammals.

A DIVERSITY OF HABITATS

Climatic changes have affected Morocco's natural flora, and the country now has a unique diversity of habitats, each with its typical species. At one end of the scale there are the arid mountain deserts and endless expanses of Sahara sands, and at the other, equally arid areas of perpetual snow on the peaks of the highest mountains. In between these extremes lie fertile valleys and coastal plains blessed with temperatures and rainfall ranging from typically Mediterranean to typically subtropical.

The plains and lowlands abound in colorful Mediterranean plants and support many varieties of fruit, vegetables, and grains. Row upon row of olive trees march in straight lines across the plains, and in many places vast tracts of nonindigenous eucalyptus have transformed the landscape. The slopes of the mountain ranges are well wooded with evergreen oak at lower levels and giant, sweet-smelling cedar higher up.

Storks nesting in the center of a town.

East and south of the Atlas Mountains the lowlands are dominated by scrubby steppe and desert vegetation—aromatic herbs, stunted trees and bushes, and most importantly the ubiquitous date palm. The desert fringes are marked by patches of coarse grass and prickly and thistly plants with many cacti.

ANIMAL LIFE

As one would expect, reptiles are fairly widespread. Lizards, chameleons, geckos, and snakes are common, and the desert is home to the fascinating sand fish—the well-camouflaged, yellow-brown Berber skink that appears to "swim" through the sand.

Mammals, especially the larger species, are relatively rare. The commonest large animals are sheep, goats, and camels, which are able to survive in generally inaccessible and virtually barren land. Red fox are also occasionally seen, and a type of monkey known as a Barbary ape frequents the cedar

Pollinating date palms.

forests. Wild boar are plentiful, and shooting them is a popular sport.

The desert fringes are inhabited by many smaller mammals such as the sand squirrel, which lives on hot rock faces, and gazelle and antelope, which graze the thorn bushes and dry grasses. The desert proper has numerous rodents like the jerboa, the desert fox, and the desert hedgehog.

IMPERIAL AND OTHER CITIES

Almost without exception, Morocco's most populous cities are located in the western lowland areas of the country. Casablanca and Rabat-Salé are on the Atlantic coast, whereas Fès and Marrakech are farther inland. Oujda, Morocco's fifth largest city, is located on an important trading crossroads— the border with Algeria.

Casablanca, Morocco's largest city and probably the largest city in North Africa, is the country's commercial capital. Next in order of size are three of the four "imperial cities"— Marrakech, Rabat-Salé, and Fès. Meknes, the last of these four, is considerably smaller.

At one time or another each of the four imperial cities served as a capital, but Rabat excepted, they were not capitals of Morocco as we know it today. Rather they served as the power base of one of the many groups who held sway after the arrival of the Arabs from the east in the late seventh century.

Fès, the oldest of the four, was founded toward the end of the eighth century and quickly became a religious and educational center. It lies in the heart of a fertile basin between the Middle Atlas and the Rif Mountains and at the crossroads of two important trade routes: one across the Sahara to Black Africa, the other eastward toward the rest of North Africa.

Casablanca is Morocco's commercial and industrial capital.

PRINCIPAL TOWNS

Estimated population figures in mid-1990. There is continuous migration from the countryside into the towns, and figures quickly become out of date.

* Casablanca - 3,210,000
* Marrakech - 1,517,000
* Rabat-Salé - 1,472,000
* Fès - 1,012,000
* Oujda - 962,000
* Kénitra - 905,000
* Tétouan and Larache - 856,000
* Safi - 845,000
* Agadir - 779,000
* Meknes - 750,000
* Tangier - 554,000

In their time the imperial cities were political, religious, and cultural centers, and they contain the majority of Morocco's treasured historic and cultural monuments.

Next in terms of age is Meknes, which is situated not far from Fès. Despite being founded in the 10th century, it did not achieve any real importance until the 17th century, when it became the capital under Sultan Moulay Ismail, ancestor of today's King Hassan II.

Similarly, Rabat has a long history. Although an important city from the 12th century onward, Rabat did not become a capital, and then only briefly, until the second half of the 18th century. In the 20th century, when the French were empowered to "protect" Morocco, it became their administrative center. Since independence, Rabat has remained the capital of modern Morocco.

The history of Marrakech, to the north of the High Atlas range, goes back to 1062. It probably started life as a town of tents around a *kasbah* ("KAHS-bah"), or fortress, in a vast palm grove but quickly became the heart of an empire stretching from Catalonia in eastern Spain to the mountains of Sudan. Its fortunes rose and fell as successive dynasties also rose and fell. Today, although time has passed it by, it is still sometimes called the capital of the "great south."

HISTORY

NO ONE KNOWS FOR SURE, but it seems likely that about one million years ago ancestors of the human species—groups of hunter-gatherer hominids—roamed the empty spaces of North Africa. What is certain, on the other hand, is that the North Africa of prehistoric times was physically quite different from the North Africa of today. Prehistoric North Africa was probably an area of dense forests and fertile plains that supported a wide range of wild game such as elephant, zebra, lion, giraffe, ostrich, and antelope. Changes in climate from around 3000 B.C. produced the arid lands of the north and the Sahara Desert of today.

Neanderthals lived in Morocco about 50,000 years ago and a specimen from this period, a young man around 16 years old, was discovered near Rabat in 1933. "Rabat man" and his relatives were followed by several kinds of Stone Age humans, who established primitive pastoral and agricultural systems in the last 10,000 years B.C.

By the time of recorded history, the area was inhabited by light-skinned tribal peoples who probably had Euro-Asiatic origins and came to be known as Berbers. Little by little the Berber tribes spread across the whole of North Africa and are now recognized as the indigenous people of Morocco. From about the sixth or seventh centuries B.C. onward they came into brief contact first with Phoenicians, then with Carthaginians, and finally with Romans. All three groups arrived in small numbers, and none had a long-term impact.

These fleeting visitors, however, were followed in the seventh century by Arab immigrants from much farther east. They too came in small numbers, but they brought with them a religion and a culture that transformed the country into the Arab state and Muslim society of today.

Opposite: **Ruins of the basilica at Volubilis date from Roman times.**

Above: **A prehistoric rock painting of a gazelle.**

EARLY DAYS

The first outsiders to establish a foothold in Berber Morocco were Phoenicians from the eastern Mediterranean. They were a maritime people, and their main objective was the creation of trading settlements along the north coast of the continent where they could set up facilities to salt fish. Carthage, in modern Tunisia, was the main focus of their interest, and they made little significant contact with the inhabitants of the Moroccan interior.

When Carthage itself became an independent state, Carthaginian traders developed the existing Phoenician settlements into prosperous towns with fish salting and preserving as major industries. They also grew wheat and grapes and minted coins. Unlike their predecessors, the Carthaginians exercised some cultural influence over the Berbers and penetrated inland, at least as far as the region around Volubilis between the Rif and the Middle Atlas mountains.

The Carthaginian empire went into decline in the face of growing Roman expansion, culminating in the sacking of Carthage in 146 B.C. In due course the Romans took over Carthaginian outposts in Morocco and incorporated them into two large provinces. But

A Volubilis mosaic.

the newcomers found themselves embroiled in constant conflict with Berber tribes. One rebellion took three years and 20,000 troops to subdue.

Although the Romans did not expand much farther south, they exploited the fertile vineyards and grainfields they had inherited and built aqueducts and reservoirs to bring water into drought-ridden areas. Streets

and private buildings, numerous sculptures and other decorations, well-preserved mosaics, and items essential to daily life such as sundials and cooking utensils have survived. Together they build up a remarkable record of the wealth of the inhabitants and the life of the times.

After 300 years of dealing with uprisings and faced with declining productivity, the Romans eventually moved their administrative centers farther east. Shortly after the middle of the third century they left Morocco for good, and the country entered a dark age about which little is known. Life in the mountains and deserts presumably went on much as before, and the coastal regions were disturbed only by the occasional incursion by Vandals and Goths sweeping south from Spain en route to northern Tunisia.

This situation came to an end around 680 with the arrival of a wave of dynamic new invaders. These were Arabs—battle-hardened pioneers from the Arabian peninsula who spread across North Africa when their expansion in other directions was temporarily blocked. Land and conquest aside, their principal aim was to convert the world to Islam, the new religion they brought from the east. A longer-term objective was the use of Morocco as a springboard for the invasion and conversion of Spain.

Roman imperial roads reached across France and Spain, and then down from Tangier, until they finally stopped at Volubilis, the empire's most remote base. The city occupied a striking site on a long, high plateau above a river valley. It was encircled by ramparts with six gates. One gate and several fragments of the walls still remain, along with large parts of the main buildings—the capitol, the basilica, and the triumphal arch.

IMPERIAL MOROCCO

Moroccan history before independence is largely a saga of shifting alliances, sporadic bids for power, and the rise and fall of various dynasties, some Arab and some with a Berber tribal basis.

With a handful of exceptions, the Moroccan ruling sultans controlled only the plains, the coastal ports, and the areas around Fès, Marrakech, Rabat, and Meknes—the so-called "imperial cities." Outside these cities, the inhabitants of the Rif and Atlas ranges and the remote deserts seldom recognized any authority beyond that of the local tribal head.

The first group to gain substantial power were the Idrissids, led by Moulay Idriss who reached Morocco in the late eighth century. He succeeded in converting enough Berbers to Islam and gained enough control, at least in the north, to set up an Arab court and kingdom.

The Idrisid dynasty was short-lived and was ousted in the 11th century by Muslim Berber rulers called the Almoravids, who moved in to rescue Moroccan Islam from the decadent habits into which they felt it had fallen. They also founded Marrakech.

When the power of the Almoravids waned, they were replaced by another Berber dynasty, the Almohads, an intensely puritanical group similarly bent on religious reform. Their best-remembered sultan was Yacoub el Mansour, who ruled from Rabat.

MEKNES—THE VERSAILLES OF MOROCCO

Moulay Ismail, the second Alouite sultan, made Meknes his capital for the 55 years of his notorious reign (1672-1727). The most tyrannical of all Moroccan rulers, he was feared for his appalling cruelty but revered for his devotion to the Islamic religion and for bringing peace and prosperity after a period of anarchy.

He was also an enthusiastic builder and created Meknes to rival the palace of Versailles in France. In its heyday the city boasted numerous mosques and bazaars, 50 palaces, 16 miles of exterior walls pierced by 20 gates, and enormous granaries to store food for his 12,000 horses.

ARABS AND ALOUITES

The Almohads were followed by another two Berber dynasties and finally, in the 16th century, by the second Arab dynasty, the Saadians, who established their base in Marrakech. The Saadians rose to power on the strength of their position as descendants of the Prophet Mohammed, and their dynasty was important because it was the first whose power did not depend on tribal alliances.

In the 17th century, when civil war erupted among rival heirs, the Saadians were ousted by the Alouites, another Arab dynasty. They too suffered from family strife, civil war, and rebellion. As the centuries passed these problems were compounded by outdated, medieval forms of government, virtual bankruptcy, and widespread discontent.

This situation left the way open for increasing intervention by foreigners and finally European occupation on the pretext of protecting trading settlements and commercial interests. By the early years of the 20th century, "imperial" Morocco was a thing of the past; tribal power had once again replaced centralized control.

The mausoleum of Moulay Ismail at Meknes.

23

CONTACTS WITH THE OUTSIDE WORLD

French colonial buildings in Casablanca.

The first Arabs arrived in Morocco in the late seventh century. They were followed at intervals by succeeding waves of Arab invaders similarly bent on conquest and conversion of the Berbers. Thereafter the increasingly mixed Arab-Berber population fiercely guarded their independence in the face of growing European interest in the territory. Initially most contact was with Spain and Portugal, and various settlements on the Moroccan coasts changed hands many times from the 15th century onward. Moroccan involvement in European politics varied according to the situation at home. At one time dissident Moroccans sought the help of Portuguese armies to settle their own quarrels. On the other hand, in the 17th century, the Alouite sultan, Moulay Ismail, felt strong enough to contemplate marriage with a French princess. The French ridiculed the idea.

THE END OF INDEPENDENCE

From the end of the Napoleonic Wars onward, Morocco fought a losing battle against European ambitions.

In later decades, with weak rulers and strife at home, Morocco became isolated until Europeans began to take a more consistent interest in their closest African neighbor. In the first half of the 19th century the French occupied territory in neighboring Algeria and inflicted a severe defeat on the Moroccan sultan when he went to the assistance of his fellow Muslims. A few years later Spain acquired Sidi Ifni on Morocco's Atlantic coast.

TANGIER, THE "INTERNATIONAL" CITY

Tangier—Morocco's 11th largest city—is the country's most cosmopolitan, atypical, and internationally famous metropolis. It is steeped in legend and its history involves interaction with Phoenicians, Carthaginians, Romans, Portuguese, and Spanish. It was even a British possession for a short period at the end of the 17th century. At the beginning of the 20th century, the city was designated an international port so that no one power would have absolute control. The arrangement was enthusiastically promoted by the British, who wished to prevent Spain from controlling both sides of the Strait of Gibraltar.

By the end of the century, Morocco was virtually bankrupt, and Spain and France used every opportunity to interfere in domestic affairs on the pretext of "protecting" their own citizens working in Morocco.

Last-minute attempts at reform, which might have saved Morocco by modernizing its antiquated forms of government, failed miserably. Meanwhile Britain, France, Germany, Spain, and Italy vied with each other to gain possession of the last few remnants of independent Africa. The European powers negotiated "spheres of influence" among themselves. Eventually the main players left were France and Spain, who made a secret agreement about how they would divide up Morocco when circumstances permitted.

In 1908, Moroccans revolted against the increasing influence of the "infidels" in their land. While the sultan was occupied with this emergency, Spain moved 90,000 troops into Melilla, claiming that they were necessary to protect Spanish workers employed in mining. This event marked the beginning of foreign occupation. Unable to assert his authority and presiding over a debt-ridden nation, in 1912 Sultan Hafid signed the Treaty of Fès, which officially brought Morocco under French and Spanish "protection." The Protectorates lasted 44 years.

The process of European advance, once started, was impossible to stop. Internal rebellions and revolts weakened Moroccan rulers and made it easier for Europeans to establish footholds on Moroccan soil.

The Spanish fort of Al Hoceima. The Spanish presence in Morocco was much less beneficial than the French. Their policies tended to provoke rebellion rather than bring peace and were instrumental in turning armed revolt into middle-class resistance.

Direct French administration sidelined the traditional ruling classes, and it is said that the point was reached when the sultan had to read French newspapers to find out what was going on in his own country.

PACIFICATION NOT PEACE

Under the terms of the Protectorate agreements, France became the dominant power in Morocco and took over what it called "useful Morocco"—the main cities on the central plains and all the territory along the Algerian border. Spain was granted two strips of territory (one along the northern coast and the other in the south, running eastward from Tarfaya), the enclave of Sidi Ifni, and parts of the Sahara Desert.

At first the terms of the Protectorate Treaty were scrupulously observed by General Lyautey, the first French Resident-General. Succeeding administrators, however, turned Morocco into a French colony in all but name. Nevertheless the French presence imposed much-needed stability, and little by little tribal rebellion was subdued. By 1934 the whole of French Morocco was under effective central control.

From the Moroccan point of view the French Protectorate had both advantages and disadvantages. Peace brought a flood of French settlers who took over the best land but also developed it in a way that had not been possible before. Roads and railways opened up the country, new towns were built, administration was modernized, the legal system reformed, and education became more widely available. However, ambitious, educated young Moroccans had no outlets for their talents.

INDEPENDENCE REGAINED

Nationalist sentiment began to make itself felt in the 1930s with the formation of the Istiqlal (Freedom) Party. French attempts to divide and rule by driving a wedge between Arabs and Berbers had the opposite effect—the two groups united in common opposition.

The French made Mohammed V sultan at the age of 17 in the hope that he would be easily controlled. However, in public speeches the young sultan spoke about the rights of the Moroccan people and their history of independence. He also signed the demand for reforms submitted by nationalist leaders.

The sultan paralyzed the government by refusing to sign legislation limiting his power, and in desperation, as rioting began, the French exiled him to Madagascar. He went quietly but refused to abdicate, an astute move that increased his popularity and stimulated nationalist fervor and spiraling violence. In November 1955, Mohammed V was allowed to return. In March of the following year the Protectorate period came to an end. Morocco was independent once more.

Mohammed V attending a festival the year before his death in 1961. His son, Hassan, present king of Morocco, leads his horse.

GENERAL HUBERT GONZALVE LYAUTEY

Lyautey, the first French Resident-General, grew to love the country he was sent to pacify and "protect." His aim was to avoid destroying age-old Moroccan traditions and habits and to take all action in the name and with the consent of the sultan and the traditional Moroccan elite.

His policy of building new, modern towns outside the ancient cities meant that the old medinas, or native towns, were left untouched and Moroccan lifestyle, as far as possible, was preserved. He was scrupulously careful not to undermine Islam or destroy any of its monuments.

Sahrawi riders in the Western Sahara. The Western Sahara continues to fight for independence in spite of Moroccan claims to the territory.

Young professionals eager to press ahead with modernizing reforms feel frustrated by the now conservative policies of the "old guard" who fought for independence.

A COUNTRY TO BE RECKONED WITH

As a modern nation, Morocco is less than 40 years old. In the short period since it regained independence, its people have had to tackle problems that older nations have had generations to address. The French left behind a well-developed industrial sector, the beginnings of a good irrigation system, and a network of roads and railways, at least in "useful Morocco." But they also left many problems: no political system from which a modern government could be developed, a lack of trained Moroccan administrators, and a wealth of ethnic and regional divisions fueled by the protracted struggle for independence.

Nonetheless, new regions are now being developed and modest health and educational facilities are being put in place. Agriculture and industry have diversified, but widespread poverty hampers progress. Morocco is still heavily in debt and in need of foreign investment.

To the outsider the numerous attempts to dethrone or assassinate King Hassan II, Morocco's second monarch, seem like ominous signs of a turbulent future. But the king has a tenacious grip on power, and his success in avoiding assassination has earned him the nickname "the Great

Survivor." In a sense it is a nickname that could be applied to the country as a whole. Life is an uphill struggle for the vast majority of Moroccans, but they are slowly forging a nation that is beginning to take its place in the modern world.

CONFLICT IN THE DESERT AND THE GREEN MARCH

The Western Sahara problem has bedeviled North African politics for the last 30 years or more. Spain took little interest in its Saharan territories until the 1960s, when valuable phosphate deposits were discovered. Thereafter there were many calls for decolonization and then for independence.

Morocco lays claim to the territory. It argues that the Saharan tribal leaders traditionally acknowledged the authority of the Moroccan sultans, but the International Court of Justice has ruled that this is not sufficient to establish sovereignty.

In November 1975 in the so-called "Green March," 350,000 Moroccan citizens walked into the Western Saharan area in support of Morocco's claim. Moroccans in the area now outnumber the original inhabitants by three to two. Meanwhile arguments continue about who should be eligible to take part in a United Nations-sponsored referendum to decide the future of the territory. Morocco has built hundreds of miles of defenses to secure the border, although 75 countries now recognize the Sahrawi Arab Democratic Republic as the legitimate government of Western Sahara.

A stamp commemorating the Green March. In the eyes of the ordinary Moroccan, the Western Sahara conflict is an emotive cause behind which the nation can unite.

GOVERNMENT

THE KINGDOM OF MOROCCO is a democratic and constitutional monarchy and an Islamic state. As a monarchy, it enjoys the distinction of being the oldest of its kind in the Muslim world. The current monarch, King Hassan II, is a member of the Alouite dynasty, which has been in power in one way or another for the last 300 years.

As a democracy, Morocco has a single-chamber parliament, but since independence no single party has been able to win sufficient parliamentary seats to muster a working majority. For this reason the monarch has considerably more power than constitutional monarchy normally implies, and it is only since 1977 that a limited democracy has been able to develop.

Local government reflects the legacy of the French Protectorate. For administrative purposes the country is divided into 39 provinces and eight urban prefectures, each with its own governor. These large units are subdivided into more than 1,500 urban and rural communes under officials known as *pashas* and *caids* ("KAA-eeds"). Similarly, the legal system is based on French law and French legal procedure, but because Morocco is a Muslim country, Islamic law is equally important.

The lack of full democracy and the feeling that the judicial system is slow, erratic, and in some cases corrupt fuels a simmering discontent especially among educated young Moroccans. However, by comparison with many other Arab or African countries, Morocco has a livelier and more diversified political life, although topics such as the role of the monarchy, Morocco's status as a Muslim country, and the policy on the disputed Western Sahara are not open to discussion.

Morocco, Tunisia, and Algeria are known collectively in the Arab world as Jeziret al-Maghreb, *or "Island of the West." Morocco's Arabic name is* El Maghreb el Aqsa, *meaning "the farthest west."*

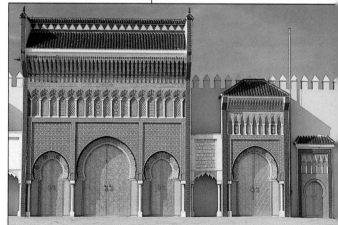

Opposite: **A guard at the Mohammed V mausoleum.**

Above: **The Royal Palace in Fès.**

The Polisario Front has been fighting for the independence of the Western Sahara. The United Nations is currently attempting to negotiate a referendum on the status of the Western Sahara.

ABOVE ALL A KINGDOM

In spite of the wording of the constitution, Morocco is more accurately described as an absolute monarchy than as a democratic state. Ever since the restoration of independence it has been governed by a sovereign with extensive powers to manipulate a weak parliamentary system.

The Moroccan parliament has a single Chamber of Representatives with 222 seats directly elected by all adults above the age of 20, and 111 seats filled by individuals chosen primarily by local councils and chambers of commerce. The monarch presides over the cabinet and appoints the prime minister, who in turn chooses the ministers, all of whom have to be approved by the sovereign. Parliamentary seats are contested by candidates from a large number of political parties ranging from the *Union Constitutionelle* and the *Mouvement Populaire* on the right, the *Rassemblement Nationale des Indépendants*, the *Mouvement Nationale Populaire,* and the *Parti National Démocratique* in the center, to various organizations on the left, the most important of which is the *Parti Istiqlal*. Although the names indicate fundamental differences, most of the parties are monarchist.

The bulk of the power resides with the right wing and the center groups, which together are often described as the loyalist parties, with the smaller left-wing and other groups forming the opposition. However, no single party has so far achieved the clear majority required to form a government, and Moroccans in general have accepted the need for a strong unifying central power in order to ensure stability. This acceptance of centralized power has its roots in traditional forms of government in the past and enables the monarchy to retain substantial control of both foreign and domestic policy.

The pattern of centralized control is repeated at the local level. Each of the provinces has an elected assembly, but the real power lies in the hands of the governor, who is appointed by the Ministry of the Interior.

In 1993 a ministry established by the king in April 1990 substantiated allegations by human rights organizations of the "disappear-ance" and detention of political activists.

THE PATH TO DEMOCRACY

Dissent is fueled by the frustrated aspirations of educated young Moroccans, widespread poverty, high unemployment, poor education, inadequate health services, and lack of housing. Criticisms, which include charges that Morocco has been a virtual one-party state for the last 20 to 30 years and sporadic allegations of corruption, have often been met with severe reprimand at best and imprisonment at worst. On occasion striking workers have been jailed. Nevertheless the signs are that Morocco is slowly advancing toward a more representative government that can implement its own policies.

Constitutional reforms in 1992 suggested that the government to be formed following elections in 1993 would more widely reflect public opinion and party support. These hopes have not materialized, but change is inevitably filtering through. For instance, domestic and international criticism of Morocco's human rights record over the last few years has recently prompted the creation of a new ministry to deal with the problems of political prisoners. At the same time, however, militant Islamic fundamentalism is ruthlessly suppressed, with offending leaders being imprisoned or placed under house arrest. In recent months, however, there have been signs of a more constructive approach. The need to tackle the social problems that contribute to the rise of violent fundamentalism has been acknowledged, and there have been attempts to win over some of the most influential militants.

KING AND CAPITAL

King Hassan II, who succeeded his father Mohammed V in 1961, is Morocco's second king since the restoration of independence in 1956. Like his father, he has a dual role as both spiritual and secular head of state.

His spiritual authority as *amir al-mu'minin* ("ah-MEER ahl-MOOK-mee-neen"), or commander of the faithful, stems from his family's claim to descent from the Prophet Mohammed. This means that despite much

King Hassan also held the post of prime minister for the first 12 years of his reign as king.

sometimes violent opposition—he has survived several assassination attempts and abortive coups—he can rely on the allegiance of the vast majority of his people. A challenge to the authority of the sovereign would be a challenge to a divine right to rule. As long as Morocco's most pressing problems are seen to be addressed, even though slowly, this authority will probably be accepted.

As the secular head of state, King Hassan is firmly in control of domestic and foreign policy. He is recognized as a pragmatic and astute politician who exercises his power with considerable skill. This has gained him widespread respect, and although not all Moroccans regard him with affection, few argue with his achievements in fostering a sense of national pride. In this context the Green March and Morocco's claim to sovereignty over the Western Sahara have played an important part. Similarly the king's long-standing role as a mediator between Israel and the Arab states and his efforts to restore good relations among Arab states in the aftermath of the

1990–91 Gulf War, which set Arab against Arab, have earned him an enviable reputation. To the world outside Morocco, King Hassan is a moderate Arab leader who has contributed substantially to world peace.

RABAT: AN ELEGANT CAPITAL

Morocco's capital is Rabat, one of the four ancient imperial cities. It is the permanent residence of the monarch and the seat of government.

Rabat is an elegant, busy city with two faces. On one hand, it has the broad avenues and abundance of trees and flowers of the modern administrative center established by the French during the Protectorate period. On the other, it has the narrow, whitewashed streets of the older town that goes back possibly to the seventh century B.C. In the 10th century A.D. it became a military garrison and the city acquired its name from *ribat* ("ree-BAT"), meaning fortified camp.

Today the heart of modern Rabat lies in the great open space and many courtyards of the *Mechouar* ("mesh-WAAR") or royal enclosure with its wealth of modern Moroccan decorative architecture. The royal palace, the royal mosque, the offices of the prime minister, the Supreme Court of Justice, and various ministries are all located here.

After Morocco regained independence, Mohammed V changed his title from sultan to king in order to demonstrate his intention of ruling along progressive lines.

THE NATIONAL FLAG

Morocco's national flag features a six-pointed Seal of Solomon in the center on a plain red background. Red flags with various emblems were long used by members of the Alouites, the dynasty that has ruled Morocco since the 17th century. The green Seal of Solomon was added in 1915 in French Protectorate times.

ECONOMY

MOROCCO DOES NOT HAVE the good fortune to be part of the oil-rich Arab world. This means that it has to spend quite heavily on fuel for its energy needs. On the other hand, it has enormous phosphate deposits and a climate that, along with land and water resources, has allowed the development of an agricultural sector that plays a vital role in both the domestic and export markets. In addition, the manufacturing sector contributes approximately 30 percent to the Gross Domestic Product (GDP), and the services sector includes a dynamic tourism industry.

Over 60 percent of Morocco's exports go to the European Community. France takes the largest proportion with 32 percent of the total, followed by Spain with 9.8 percent. Other important trading partners are India with 6 percent, Japan with 4.9 percent, the United States with 3.7 percent, and Libya with 3.3 percent.

The economy is steadily expanding. The average annual growth rate between 1985 and 1991 was 4.6 percent but severe droughts in 1992 and 1993 adversely affected agricultural production and reduced this figure. There are also other problems. A young population means that hundreds of thousands of new jobs are needed every year. For those who are employed, wages are low. Many who cannot find employment at home, or sufficiently well paid employment, go in search of better salaries elsewhere. Last but by no means least, there is a significant "informal sector" of the economy, which escapes taxation and government control and frequently involves illegal activities.

Opposite: **A dentist looks for a new customer on the Djemm el'Fna in Marrakech.**

Above: **Olives are an important export.**

FROM CENTRALIZED CONTROL TO PRIVATIZATION

A vendor in a wool market.

Today's buzz word in Morocco is "privatization." In the 1960s, in the early days of independence, there were high hopes for a liberal economic approach, but instead Morocco found itself attempting to control economic development through central planning. In succeeding years, therefore, public utilities, dam and irrigation schemes, major chemical industries, the production of tea, sugar, and tobacco, and many other crucial concerns were placed under state control. Similarly, certain economic services such as the marketing of agricultural and other produce abroad were centrally coordinated to the benefit of those concerned.

Initially all went fairly well, but after a while the good beginning lost momentum, leading to a weakened economic situation. Oil prices rose dramatically and drought adversely affected agriculture and the production of hydroelectricity. A continually rising birthrate aggravated unemployment and put a great strain on health and education facilities, and on Morocco's ability to feed itself. Conflicts such as the controversy over the Western Sahara were another drain on the treasury.

Heavily in debt, Morocco applied to the International Monetary Fund, the World Bank, and other international bodies for assistance and set about implementing various policies that, it is hoped, will eventually remedy the situation. Structural reforms, including a gradual reduction in public expenditure and a general process of liberalization and diversification of the economy, got under way in 1986. There have been many setbacks, but progress is slowly being made and essential foreign investment is growing.

Numerous enterprises in agriculture, in the food, banking, and financial sectors, in textiles, leather, and other areas of industrial production, and in tourism and other services have been privatized. State assets in hotels, sugar production, road transport, petroleum distribution, petrochemicals, housing, textiles, and cement have been sold, and Morocco is now committed to free-market policies with privatization of all but a few strategic industries and key public utilities and services.

IMPORTS

Morocco's climate often affects its ability to produce enough food, especially cereals and dairy items. For this reason, it has to import substantial quantities of food and drink along with tobacco and sugar. The lack of fuel for energy means that crude oil has to be imported.

Food, drink, tobacco, energy, and lubricants account for about a third of Morocco's expenditure on imports. Capital goods, such as raw materials and machinery, account for around a quarter of the import bill, and semi-finished products absorb a similar amount.

The food bill may decrease as food production increases, but a drop in the fuel bill is unlikely. Morocco has only limited natural energy resources—a little coal, a little oil, and some natural gas. The expansion of hydroelectric output is limited because water supplies are severely affected by periodic droughts. Demand for electricity is expected to double every 10 years, and Morocco is currently importing electric power from the Algerian grid.

Saudi Arabia supplies 25 percent of Morocco's imported oil. The United Arab Emirates supply 19%, 13% comes from Iran, and 5% each is from Libya and Cameroon.

The Ben el-Ovidame Dam provides hydroelectric power.

Farms are small and much of the work is done by hand.

Climate and location ensure that Moroccan fruit and vegetables are ready a few weeks earlier than similar crops in southern Europe, providing a competitive edge.

A THRIVING AGRICULTURAL SECTOR

Agriculture plays a pivotal role in the economy despite the fact that farms are small in size, averaging less than 12 acres each. Furthermore, few small farmers have electricity or running water, and communications in outlying areas leave much to be desired. Another worry is that the average age of farmers is over 50, and between two-thirds and three-quarters are illiterate. Despite these disadvantages, the agricultural sector provides employment for close to 40 percent of the nearly 10 million work force.

Farm products are responsible for 17 percent of total exports, and the industry is expanding both in terms of products and new markets. Primary production of fresh fruit and vegetables is complemented by related industries focusing on animal feed, fruit and vegetable processing, dairy products, and sugar byproducts.

Fertile plains and plateaus, a variety of temperate and semiarid climates, and a long growing season permit the production of a wide range of vegetables and fruit. Unfortunately, production levels tend to be erratic because of climatic conditions, especially periodic droughts, but investment in irrigation programs is slowly bringing the problem under control.

IRRIGATION PROGRAMS

Morocco has 19.25 million acres of arable land, but only two million are constantly irrigated. These two million, however, employ one in three of all agricultural workers. They also account for three quarters of all agricultural exports and for 90 percent of their value. The figures amply demonstrate the advantages of irrigation, and steps are currently being taken to develop the full potential of numerous underground water supplies. An ambitious project known as the Program of National Irrigation for the Year 2000 aims to refurbish or modernize equipment and irrigate all land within reach of existing dams, or those under construction, before the end of the century.

Meanwhile, financial measures have also been taken to counteract the effects of drought and protect the industry.

In 1984, after three water-starved years, King Hassan decreed that farming would be exempt from taxes until the year 2000—a bold concession that has acted as a welcome boost to the industry as a whole.

The programs already in place have had remarkable results, particularly in making diversification possible. Citrus fruits and tomatoes previously provided the bulk of exports, but in the 1990s Morocco is successfully opening up markets for its potatoes, squash, winter melons, strawberries, artichokes, peas, chilis, green beans, and cut flowers in the European Community, especially Spain and France.

FISHING

Fishing, along with processing and canning operations, employs more than 100,000 people and in 1992 accounted for 13.7 percent of total exports. The seas off the country's 2,180 miles of coastline are rich in sardines, and Morocco is among the world's leading suppliers of this commodity. Other seafood products include lobster and swordfish, tuna, and several types of shellfish.

The busy fishing port of Agadir.

VALUABLE MINERAL RESOURCES

Currently Morocco supplies about one-third of all phosphates used worldwide. It is also the largest phosphates exporter in the world and owns three-quarters of the world's phosphate reserves. At present production levels, it is estimated that this represents enough phosphates to meet total demand for 1,000 years. Deposits of other minerals—iron ore, cobalt, manganese, lead, zinc, copper, fluorite, and anthracite—are useful but pale into insignificance by comparison.

The phosphate industry today, together with expanding related industries like the production of phosphoric acid and chemical fertilizers, is a mainstay of the economy and accounts for about one-quarter of all exports.

   In the 1970s, after the spectacular rise in the price of oil, phosphate prices also rose, and Morocco invested heavily in developing this valuable industry. When the price of oil fell a few years later, the price of phosphates also came down. This collapse, along with the cost of importing oil and the effects of severe drought, forced Morocco into debt. In the long term, however, the investment has proved worthwhile.

CASABLANCA—ECONOMIC CAPITAL

Efficient, streamlined Casablanca is Morocco's busiest port and the center of business and banking activities. Well over half the country's industry is located on its outskirts, and the main street boasts impressive skyscrapers.

   Despite its modern appearance, the city has a long and turbulent history going back to prehistoric times. In the 12th century it was known as Anfa. Subsequently it became a refuge for pirates and was twice destroyed by the Portuguese, once in 1468 and again in 1515.

   In 1755, the town was destroyed again, this time by the Lisbon earthquake. When the town was rebuilt it was called Dar el Beida, Arabic for "white house." Later, when the Spaniards were authorized to trade in the city, they changed its name to Casa Blanca—Spanish for "white house."

MANUFACTURING INDUSTRIES

The production of textiles and leather goods is responsible for another 20 percent of exports. About one-third of all industrial workers are employed in spinning, weaving, knitting, and the production of clothing and shoes. Sophisticated textile mills turn out large quantities of ready-made clothing and accessories for world markets.

Morocco has long been known for the quality of its leather goods. Clothing is the largest earner, followed by knitted goods, carpets, shoes, and finally various fabrics.

Meanwhile, mechanical and engineering industries are growing steadily in importance. Automobile, truck, and other vehicle parts and accessories are produced, and vehicles are assembled for several international automotive companies. Another sector builds and exports household goods such as refrigerators, gas heaters, and water meters, in addition to pumps and irrigation equipment.

The electronics industry is similarly expanding thanks to the existence of a large pool of skilled workers. Production includes electronic equipment, such as computers, semiconductors, transistors, electric cables, radios and television, electronic games, telecommunications equipment, and electronic assembly lines for other industries.

The tanneries in Fès. Fès is renowned for its infamous, stinking tanneries and its blue-and-white pottery.

Such prestigious companies as Cartier, Christian Dior, and Ted Lapidus have their designer leather and textile products made in Morocco.

SO MUCH TO SEE AND DO

For tourists, especially those who come from Europe in search of sunshine and a different culture, Morocco has become a popular destination. The tourist trade is a flourishing business.

The beauty and variety of the landscape is a feast for the senses. Oases spring from the desert, wildflowers bloom in mountain valleys, and snowclad peaks tower above ancient cities. For beach lovers, sand, sun, and sea are available along the rocky Mediterranean coast and along the Atlantic seaboard, where fine resorts overlook glorious bays and vast stretches of golden sand. There is also much to attract the sports-minded visitor, especially golf and skiing.

An Agadir beach cafe draws tourists in search of sun and scenery.

Morocco is a treasure house of exotic sights and sounds. The four imperial cities are filled with ancient mosques and palaces. Local dress and customs are colorful, and the bustling markets overflow with handcrafted souvenirs.

Given such attractions, it is not surprising that tourism is Morocco's fastest expanding industry. The country is seen as exciting but safe. Even so, for two main reasons, it has fewer visitors than might be expected. First, in the main cities at least, foreign visitors are frequently harassed by unofficial guides and unscrupulous taxi drivers. Secondly, accommodations have not yet attained the standards the international vacationer now demands.

To a large extent these problems are the result of Morocco's isolation from the outside world until fairly recent times. Modern Western standards and aggressive marketing techniques are only slowly being learned. Similarly, the need for adequate backup in terms of good accommodation, facilities, information, and communications has not yet been fully comprehended. On the other hand, isolation has had advantages. More than anywhere else in North Africa, Morocco has retained old traditions and lifestyles; these alone are potent tourist attractions.

MOROCCAN ADVENTURES

The lonely expanses of Morocco's vast interior are the focus of adventure tours. Increasing numbers of visitors seek exciting excursions trekking through remote areas, sometimes accompanied by a mule train and often sleeping in tents. Farther south, camel and Jeep safaris reveal the strange beauty of the desert and the pre-Saharan valleys. Whitewater rafting also caters to those who crave the thrill of speed and danger.

The *souk* ("sook," or market) in Marrakech is the center of much economic activity.

THE INFORMAL SECTOR

Morocco has a traditional and flourishing informal sector that provides employment for hundreds of thousands of workers. There are various reasons for its existence. Many businesses conceal their activities because labor laws make it difficult and expensive to fire employees. Some industrialists feel that government inspectors are harsh in their treatment of entrepreneurs; this encourages people to cheat. Low salaries also create problems: those who should enforce various duties and taxes often have little incentive to do so.

Figures collected in 1988 and thought to be still valid indicate that this type of casual, unregulated business provides 450,000 jobs in manufacturing alone. The industries most affected by this phenomenon are clothing and upholstery, food processing, and the transportation of goods.

Unfortunately, many of the activities within this sector of the economy are also outside the law, such as the flourishing production of *kif*, or hashish as it is more widely known outside Morocco. The trade is calculated by some to account for nearly a third of Europe's annual

46

KIF IN THE RIF

Kif—the cut and dried leaves of a member of the sisal plant family—grows in the rugged Rif mountains in terraced plantations. It is illegal to cultivate, sell, use, or transport kif, but smoking it has long been part of Moroccan life, and the practice is hard to eradicate.

The process of turning the mild kif into the more potent (because more concentrated) hashish has made many Riffian farmers who were previously working at subsistence level relatively rich. As elsewhere, however, it is not the growers but the drug barons for whom the trade proves most lucrative.

consumption and to be worth around $2 billion a year.

There is also a substantial smuggling industry. Illegal imports through the two Spanish enclaves in the north (Ceuta and Melilla) include alcohol, which retails at about one-third of its price in Casablanca, and desirable and otherwise expensive consumer items such as stereos and computers. Large numbers of cars, perhaps up to 40,000 a year, are stolen in Europe and smuggled in for sale, while fish caught by Moroccan fishermen are sold on the high seas in exchange for foreign currency.

Many home industries suffer as a result of these illegal activities, and the government loses significant amounts of revenue. Even more serious perhaps are the effects on future expansion of the Moroccan economy. Foreign investment is essential, but until these problems are addressed, potential investors are hesitant to put their trust in Morocco.

It is estimated that a quarter of all hotel business and no less than 19 percent of all activities grouped under the general name of repairs fall within the informal sector.

MOROCCANS

IN DAYS GONE BY, the inhabitants of northern Africa, especially large parts of modern Algeria and Morocco, were known to the Europeans as Moors. As groups of Arabs moved into the area from the east and began to mingle with the indigenous Berber people, "Moor" was used to describe people of mixed Berber and Arab race. The name came from the Greek word *mauros* but was probably a word of North African origin. In more recent times the French called the country *le Maroc* and its people *les marrocains* ("mah-roh-KA")—hence today's Morocco and Moroccans.

In the Middle Ages Moors were commonly thought to be negroid in appearance. By the 16th century, enough was known about the people of North Africa and their increasing intermingling with various peoples from Black Africa for Shakespeare to present his Prince of Morocco in *The Merchant of Venice* as "tawny," while two other Shakespearean Moors are black. A variety of peoples make up today's Moroccans, including Berbers, Arabs, and Black Africans. Most Moroccans are of mixed stock.

The Moorish character has been misunderstood due to ignorance of the culture. History reveals the Moroccans to be a people of rugged determination and courage, tolerant of other Islamic sects and of other religions. Meanwhile, Moroccans' generous hospitality and regard for family values are almost legendary.

POPULATION FACTS AND FIGURES

The vast majority of Moroccans are Arab, Berber, or mixed race people. There is also a significant Black minority that has grown up following centuries of trade with countries of Black Africa. Most Black Moroccans live in the southern areas of the country and in Marrakech and Meknes. Finally, there is a Jewish community of about 10,000 and a foreign community that has dwindled from around 500,000 at independence to 60,000 today. These people are mainly French and Spanish nationals, many of whom are teachers or technicians, and a small number of Italians.

The population is concentrated in the western part of Morocco on the fertile plains and in the coastal areas. Most industrial and economic activity is also located here. So too are all the large cities, except for Oujda in the northeast.

According to the 1982 census (the latest held in Morocco) the population, including residents in the disputed Western Sahara, numbered nearly 20,500,000. In 1993, official estimates put the number at between 25 and 26 million. This increase reflects a high average growth rate. In contrast to the aging populations of many European countries, nearly half of Morocco's population is under 20 and about 70 percent is less than 25.

The huge number of young people puts a great strain on the economy. Morocco desperately needs skilled workers and executives, so about one-quarter of the national budget is spent on education, but there are still not

The Moroccan population is overwhelmingly young.

A crowd fills the square in Marrakech. The growing population has posed problems for Morocco.

enough facilities for everyone. About half of all adult men (and an even greater number of women) can neither read nor write, and this traps great numbers of workers in low-paid, casual work.

Some people regard family planning as part of the answer to the problem, but in the 1960s suggestions that family size could be controlled were rejected on the grounds that contraception runs counter to Muslim culture. In recent years the king himself has spoken publicly about the need for family planning. Today, ideas that at one time would have been considered antireligious are being discreetly aired and slowly accepted.

Large parts of Morocco are sparsely populated. Ninety percent of the population lives north of a diagonal line drawn between the plain surrounding the Sous River near Agadir in the southwest and Oujda in the north east.

MOROCCANS ABROAD

More than 1.7 million Moroccans live and work abroad because of lack of employment and low wages at home. There are 720,000 Moroccans in France, 190,000 in the Netherlands, 170,000 in Belgium, while Italy, Spain, and Germany together play host to another 200,000.

In Africa, Libya and Algeria have a total Moroccan population of 220,000, and smaller numbers are scattered in various Muslim countries around the world.

Berber women frequently tattoo their faces.

In general, all Moroccan Berbers are members of one of three tribes—the Riffians in the north, the Chleuhs in the Middle and High Atlas regions, and the Soussi in the southwest. Each tribe has its own distinct dialect.

BERBERS—THE INDIGENOUS PEOPLE

The indigenous people of Morocco are the Berbers who, since the beginning of recorded history, are known to have lived in largely scattered tribes in the areas of North Africa that are now Morocco, Algeria, Tunisia, Libya, and Egypt. Little is known for certain about Berber origins, but the high cheekbones, fair coloring, and occasional green or blue eyes found among them suggest that they have European connections or that they are Euro-Asiatics. In any case, they were never a single, homogeneous group, but a collection of tribes living in different areas, with different lifestyles and languages, and with diverse physical and cultural characteristics.

The Berbers have lived alongside people of Arab origin for around 1,200 years. They intermarried with them and were converted to the Islamic religion. A very large number also adopted Arabic as their language. Even so, the Berbers claim that they have never been conquered. It is perhaps more accurate to say that the Phoenicians and the Carthaginians

BERBERS FROM BARBARY!

The Arabs were probably responsible for coining the word "Berber" to describe the indigenous peoples of North Africa. It is likely they adopted the word from the Greek *bárbaros,* which was used to mean "those who are foreign," that is, not Greek. Among the Arabs, Berber indicated people who were not of Arab origin, and for many centuries Barbary was the name given to Berber-occupied parts of North Africa. *Bárbaros* is also the root of "barbarian" and "barbaric" because the highly civilized Greeks felt that people who did not speak their language were at best uncivilized and at worst savage.

had little interest in doing so and that the Romans had only limited success in subduing a few tribes in the interior.

In the seventh century, when small numbers of Arabs began to arrive, the Berbers were impressed by the Arabs' desire for expansion and their missionary zeal. Little by little the various indigenous tribes were converted to Islam, but even within this framework the Berbers retained their power for about 500 years.

A succession of Muslim Berbers ruled a number of independent kingdoms. They included camel-riding desert nomads, quiet farming people from the High and Anti-Atlas, and tribes that edged in slowly from the empty area between present-day Taza and Algeria in search of better pasture for their flocks. Thereafter, newly arriving Arab groups gained the upper hand and displaced the Berbers as the dominant power in Morocco.

It is difficult to say what proportion of the total population is Berber. Perhaps 60 percent have Berber blood, but only about one-third habitually speak a Berber language rather than Arabic, which is the national language.

Berbers today are moving to the cities; they also form the bulk of the 1.7 million Moroccans forced by unemployment to seek work outside the country.

By and large today's Moroccan Berbers live in the mountainous countryside, but in recent years many have moved into urban areas.

The traditional fez is rarely worn today.

ARABS FROM THE EAST

The name "Arab" is loosely given to people whose native language is Arabic. By and large, Moroccan Arabs are descendants of people of true Arab stock who intermarried with the indigenous Berbers.

The first Arabs arrived in Morocco in the late seventh century. After the death of the Prophet Mohammed in 632, his followers embarked on careers of conquest in search of land and booty, and filled with missionary zeal, they sought to carry the message of their new religion far and wide. After conquests to the east of Arabia, they turned westward and in particular to the lands stretching along the north coast of Africa.

In 683 Oqba ben Nafi led his army into what is now Morocco and spurred his horse into the Atlantic Ocean, shouting triumphantly that only the sea prevented him from carrying his conquest any farther. He called the African territory he conquered *el Maghreb*, meaning the West, and Morocco *el Maghreb el-Aqsa* or the farthest West. Today Morocco, Algeria, and Tunisia are still known as the Maghreb countries.

By 711 most of northern Africa was under Muslim control, although only about 100,000 Arabs had been involved in the conquest of this vast tract of the continent. In the next five centuries waves of relatively small

Originally the name "Arab" applied only to people living in the Arabian Peninsula, but today it describes around 100 million people living in the Middle East and North Africa and large minorities in other parts of the world.

54

groups of Arabs reached Morocco and settled there. Some were dissidents who moved westward to escape the fighting over who should succeed Mohammed as the leader of Islam; others were refugees fleeing violent disputes over the interpretation of the Koran—the Muslim holy book.

The style of conquest varied. One group created Fès, the first of the four imperial cities, and established Arab authority in the north of the country, but another group was likened to "an army of locusts destroying everything in their path." Various communities settled peacefully along the northern edge of the Sahara Desert or in the southern coastal plains. Mostly they played no major role in Moroccan life until the middle of the 16th century, when turbulence among the Berbers brought them to power.

Arabs were never numerous, but the Berbers adopted their religion, and many adopted their language. Life in the large cities where the Arabs congregated was primarily Arab and Islamic in style, and Berbers in many parts of the countryside found their sedentary way of life undermined by the arrival of more dynamic, nomadic tribes. Only the mountain areas escaped this disruption in traditional lifestyles.

It is difficult to distinguish Arabs from Berbers.

AN ARAB NATION?

Moroccans are regarded as Arabs in an Arab country for two reasons: the monarch claims direct descent from the Prophet Mohammed, and the people mostly speak Arabic. Although Morocco is not racially an Arab nation, Moroccans have an emotional identification with the Arab world.

Moroccans have long been a people of mixed race. In their veins there runs the blood of many races—the indigenous Berbers, the relatively small numbers of Arabs who settled in Morocco over a period of around six centuries, slaves imported from Black Africa, and immigrants from Spain who were themselves a mixture of Arab, Berber, and native Iberians. Physical appearance is not a reliable guide. It is virtually impossible, and with a few exceptions, meaningless, to distinguish Arab from Berber. Today the people of Morocco regard themselves primarily as Moroccans, then as Arabs.

"Morocco is ... reviewing its identity. Geographically it is part of North Africa, but emotionally it is strongly tied to the Arab world. Devotionally it belongs to Islam, but economically it has decided that it wishes to be linked to Europe."

-The Financial Times

THE REAL DIVIDE

Even so, an Arab-Berber divide does exist, but it is geographic rather than racial. Broadly speaking, there are two groups of Moroccans—those who live in urban areas and those who live in the countryside. The Arabic speaking majority is concentrated in the lowlands and in the cities, although there are isolated groups of mainly Arab people in areas that are otherwise predominantly Berber. The Berbers (that is, those who speak mainly Berber), on the other hand, generally inhabit the poorer mountain areas. They account for between 35 and 40 percent of the population. The proportion is likely to fall in years to come because, little by little, they are leaving the countryside and drifting into the towns in search of better-paid work and better educational and health facilities.

In the 1930s, when the French attempted to set Arabs against Berbers in order to facilitate French control, the plan misfired. This attempt at manipulation by a common enemy brought the two together and Arabs openly prayed, "Oh God, separate us not from our Berber brothers."

Opposite and left: **The real division is between rural and urban dwellers.**

LIFESTYLE

EVERY MOROCCAN DRINKS mint tea. It is the national drink—an amber-colored, fragrant liquid, served piping hot in small glasses, and heavily loaded with sugar. It is refreshing and thirst-quenching even when the weather is stiflingly hot. At other times, on cool or damp days, a glass of hot tea is a warming and revitalizing refreshment.

Mint tea is jokingly nicknamed "Moroccan whiskey," but it plays a more essential role in Moroccan life than whiskey in its native Scotland. Few business deals are concluded without several glasses of tea, and the making and serving of tea is a focal point of Moroccan hospitality. Its preparation is both serious and leisurely and emphasizes the importance placed on hospitality as a part of daily life. A guest invited to make the tea is conscious of being made very welcome and highly honored.

The tea-making ritual is elaborate and dignified. The necessary implements are a round-bellied teapot with a conical lid, small glasses, and three boxes containing respectively green tea, chunks of white sugar, and sprigs of mint. The tea is put in the pot, and boiling water is added along with large quantities of sugar and handfuls of mint.

The liquid is left to infuse for a while, then a little is poured out for sampling—an action often carried out with all the concentration of a connoisseur tasting wine. The tea is then poured back into the pot and more sugar or mint added if required. Finally, it is ready. The tea maker raises the pot with a flourish, holds it high above the glasses, and fills each one to the brim.

Opposite: **A seminomadic baby has a bath.**

Below: **Tea was introduced into Morocco by British merchants in 1854, when the Crimean War forced them to look for new markets. Moroccans adopted the new drink with great enthusiasm but adapted it to suit their sweet tooth and flavored it with fresh mint.**

Moroccans enjoy taking their time over activities such as a picnic.

Morocco has 27 airports, 10 of which are international. The national airline, Royal Air Maroc, flies both internally and overseas, and has services to Europe, the Middle East, Africa, and North America.

A DIFFERENT SENSE OF TIME

The Moroccan delight in offering hospitality implies a certain attitude toward time. The making of tea takes time, a celebratory meal takes time to prepare and time to eat, and conversing courteously with guests or with business colleagues is not something to be hurried. Buying and selling also require a generous investment of time.

In general, Moroccans have not yet been contaminated by the frenetic pace of modern life typical of the most developed parts of the West. They proceed on the assumption that when God made time, he made plenty of it! The completion of a business deal, adequate rainfall, or the solutions to one's problems—all these things will come in the goodness of time and, most importantly, provided God is willing. The phrase *Insha'Allah* ("in-SHAH-lah"), which translates as "If God wills" or "God willing," appears over and over again in conversations and even in announcements of facts.

This does not mean that life in Morocco is totally relaxed. On the contrary, although doing business is considerably more time-consuming than in most developed countries, the Moroccan businessperson is efficient, and business, when necessary, can be fast and furious.

TRANSPORTATION

Mile upon mile of dirt tracks and rough trails wind across lonely mountain and desert terrain, but there is also a network of good roads that serve the urban and western part of the country and link them with more remote and distant centers of population. Freeways are still rare—the only existing stretch runs between Casablanca and Rabat—but more are planned and some are already under construction.

Morocco possesses excellent communications systems—probably the best in North Africa. An efficient rail network complements the road network and connects the main towns of the north, the coast, and Marrakech, while the international airport at Casablanca links Morocco to the outside world.

Public transport is good and not outrageously expensive for the average Moroccan. The very poorest have to make do with their donkeys and mules; the slightly better off use one of the various bus systems or "grand taxis" if there is a little money to spare. "Grands," or collective taxis, are usually big Peugeot or Mercedes models that run on regular routes. Three or four passengers squash into the back, and another one or two share the front seat with the driver.

In the cities, the commonest form of transportation after the public bus is the ubiquitous little taxi. They are easily recognized by their color (yellow in Marrakech, for instance), and their roof racks with the often decoratively inscribed words *Petit Taxi*. In the countryside, the roads demand more robust vehicles such as trucks, pickups, and Land Rovers—in short, any form of transportation that can survive the bone-shaking experience of dirt and rock-strewn roads.

The Moroccan who is wealthy enough to own motorized transport is most likely to have a moped of some kind. These are said to outnumber cars by 500 to one.

A busy street in Casablanca.

61

In the medina, the sublime may be hidden behind high walls, but it exists alongside the mundane and the squalid.

CITY LIFE

At present 45 percent of Moroccans live in the towns, but in the foreseeable future it is expected that the urban and rural populations will be about equal, with around 13 million in the countryside and 13 million more in the expanding towns and cities.

Today virtually every large town or city with any degree of history has three distinct parts—the *medina* ("may-DEE-nah"), the modern town, and the *souk*. Medinas are Arab-built, often medieval areas, usually a labyrinthine maze of narrow, winding streets and passages filled with small workshops and humble homes. At worst, they are slums populated by the the poor. At best they are ancient walled cities humming with vitality, though often lacking in basic amenities.

In the medinas, light filters in through trellises above crowded lanes. Here carts laden with goods jostle for room with children carrying trays of dough to the bakeries, gaggles of brightly dressed women, some veiled some not, and men in *djellabas* ("jeh-LAH-bahs"). The air is filled with the sounds of chatter, the cries of beggars, vendors shouting their wares, much hawking and spitting, and the clatter of hammers in the metal workshops. In the midst of all this din the gentle clip-clop of hooves on cobbles can hardly be heard, but harsh cries of *balak!* ("BAA-lek," or "look out!") alert passersby to the danger of being crushed against the wall by an overloaded donkey or run down by a tradesperson in a hurry.

Separate quarters are devoted to the making and selling of different items—embroidered slippers, jewelry, teapots and trays, carved wooden furniture, carpets, and rugs. Workshops, and the entrances to homes, are often little more than holes in the wall. The same may be true of an exquisite mosque or a grand palace—treasure houses of fine stucco and woodcarving, somber mosaic, and shady, serene patios with fountains and flowers.

Medinas also include souks, or market areas where Moroccans shop for meat, fruit, vegetables, and other foodstuffs, as well as for household goods, spices, perfumes, cosmetics, aphrodisiacs, magic potions, and fresh mint to flavor their tea.

FRENCH-STYLE MODERN TOWNS

It was fortunate for Morocco that the first resident-general of the French Protectorate was an enlightened military officer sympathetic toward the culture of the people he was sent to "protect." The country desperately needed modern forms of government and administration, but rather than pull down or otherwise adapt existing structures, Lyautey organized the building of new towns outside the medinas.

Many of Morocco's rich—few though they are—have moved to these quiet suburbs and have set up home in whitewashed, flower-smothered Mediterranean-style villas, or modern houses and blocks of flats with neat and well-kept gardens.

The "new towns," as they are still called, have wide streets, grand boulevards that often radiate from a central square, leafy suburbs lined with orange and jacaranda trees, and elegant cafés.

Berber families washing potatoes in the Setti Fatma Valley.

RURAL LIFE

Outside the big cities, people are congregated in small, dusty towns. In Berber country, homes or even whole villages are *kasbahs*—fortified buildings constructed from palm-tree fibers and compressed mud-clay from the river banks—a mixture known as *pisé* ("PEE-say"). Elsewhere there are villages carved into or clinging onto the rock of mountainsides, virtually indistinguishable from their natural background. Villages in the north are often clusters of whitewashed houses with tiled staircases and small windows with wrought-iron grilles. The desert fringes and remote mountain valleys are dotted with the black tents of nomadic tribes.

WEALTH AND WORK

As in so many developing countries, Morocco has a few rich and many poor, with a slowly emerging middle class. In general, there is a big difference between town and country incomes, and living conditions and amenities in country areas are usually worse than those in urban areas. It is significant that the loneliest villages are occupied primarily by women, children, and the old because the able-bodied men have migrated to the towns in search of work or better-paid work. In addition, every town has its sad quota of beggars—the blind, the maimed, and emaciated women with hands outstretched for a few *dirhams* to feed their children.

For many people, regardless of where they work, conditions are hard despite the fact that local labor laws are based on International Labor Organization recommendations. Working hours, for both sexes, are controlled to a maximum of a certain number of hours per day or week; all workers must have weekly rest periods of at least 24 consecutive hours and are entitled to paid holidays according to their length of service. It is unfortunate that those in the informal sector can fall through the safety net that these regulations are intended to provide. Another problem is that the physical working conditions can often be appalling, especially in the medinas where numerous health risks make for a short, hard life.

An estimated 20 percent of the workforce is unemployed or underemployed. Both situations cause poverty and foment discontent. For lack of other employment, well educated students, for instance, are forced to work as unofficial guides, and the search for work drives 1.7 million Moroccans overseas. Social security provisions to alleviate these problems include temporary food and job programs but extend only to a small percentage of the workforce.

WAGES AND SALARIES

For those lucky enough to have a job, the pay is low. In 1993, for example, the official, guaranteed minimum wage was only six dirhams per hour. Other hourly wage rates, including efficiency bonuses, were:

Unskilled laborer	6.18-6.25 dirhams
Specialized worker	6.90-8.36 dirhams
Semi-qualified worker	8.32-8.88 dirhams
Qualified worker	9.60-11.70 dirhams
Team leader	13.01-14.78 dirhams

Monthly salaries for supervisors, and for engineers and higher staff, are in the range 2,489-3,393 and 6,588-10,980 dirhams respectively. The differentials may not seem great, but because salaries are generally low they tend to encourage corruption, moonlighting, and tax evasion.

The current exchange rate is 9.22 dirhams to $1 US.

A classroom in the Draa Valley.

Approximately one- quarter of the country's budget is spent on educating its young population.

HEALTH

Ten years ago the average Moroccan who survived infancy could expect to live 60 years. Today, the figure has crawled up to 62, but it is still low compared to other countries with similar per capita incomes. In terms of stability, tolerance, and certain areas of economic progress, Morocco is often compared favorably with its neighbors, but its health record is not so good. In Tunisia, for instance, life expectancy is considerably higher— around 70 years—and the infant mortality rate is only 43 per 1,000 births. In Morocco the figure is 65 per 1000 births—an improvement on the 1985 figure of 85, but still not impressive.

Health facilities are patchy. People in rural areas and the urban poor are badly served and in particular need access to clean, safe water. Malnutrition is also common in both these groups. Medical services and personnel tend to be concentrated in urban areas, with the exception of the remote Western Sahara. Here, in what most people would consider the back of beyond, hospitals and health centers have been built and equipped to high standards, and medicine and operations are free. This is all part of a policy to reinforce Morocco's claim to the territory by attracting Moroccans to the area and making it desirable to stay.

EDUCATION

The emphasis on education is relatively recent and is bedeviled by many problems—cost, lack of teachers, lack of buildings, remote communities, and an ever-expanding population. Education is compulsory between the ages of 7 and 13 and includes five years of primary school followed by three or four years of secondary education or training in a technical school.

By no means do all Moroccan children go to school. As in the case of health facilities and for the same reason, people in the Western Sahara fare better than their compatriots elsewhere. In El Aaiún, the provincial capital, 90 percent of children of school age attend school. In other parts of Morocco, especially in small, isolated communities or where family poverty means children have to work alongside their parents, the figure is much lower. Traditional priority is still often given to boys.

Despite so many problems, however, increasing numbers of students pass through the education system and enroll in institutes of higher education and local universities to study medicine, law, business, liberal arts, the sciences, and mining. A lucky few receive financial assistance to study overseas, usually in France. However, talented students, returning home eager for employment and the opportunity to put into practice new ideas absorbed overseas, are often frustrated in reaching their goals.

A large proportion of the older generations cannot read or write. Illiteracy in the countryside is worse than in the towns, and everywhere the figures are worse for women.

In 1991 only 45 people in every 100 could read.

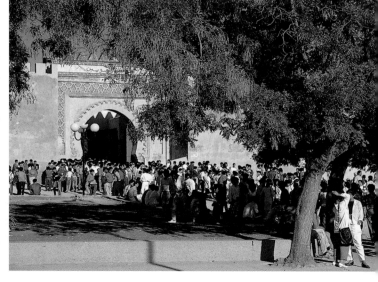

Students outside the University of Fès. In February 1994 there were violent clashes between radical Islamic and left-wing students at Fès University. Dozens of students were arrested, and courses at the university were suspended indefinitely.

Family life is of great importance to Moroccans.

THE CORNERSTONE OF SOCIETY

Family life is regarded as the cornerstone of society and great emphasis is placed on family values, family cohesion, and hospitality. A wedding, the birth of a child, and the circumcision of a young boy are all cause for much rejoicing, celebration, and ritual.

There was a time when all marriages were arranged, with eligible young men and women obediently marrying according to their parents' choice. The woman was by and large a chattel to be sold at the highest price. Quite possibly neither party had much contact with the other before the first stage in the marriage negotiations—the formal agreement that was signed a year or two before the ceremony.

Today educated Moroccans increasingly prefer and are able to choose their own partners, and many opt for a simple ceremony rather than the elaborate 15-day event of the past, with its strict protocol. Also disappearing to a large extent is the presence of a third party on the wedding night to verify the bride's virginity and the consummation of the marriage.

Moroccan law permits polygamy. In accordance with Islamic practice, a Moroccan man may take up to four wives, provided he can show that he is a genuinely practicing Muslim. However, the situation is changing as more emancipated Moroccan women become less willing to accept this.

Another factor discouraging polygamy is the question of cost. A wedding is an expensive affair made even more expensive by the traditional gifts presented to the bride's family. The rising cost of marriage, along with recession and reduced employment possibilities, means that young people are having to marry later than they formerly did.

HOUSE AND HOME—AN INTENSELY PRIVATE WORLD

"Privacy" is the key word in Moroccan home life. Homes are inward-looking. Rooms typically open onto a central courtyard, and the largely blank exterior walls hide patios and gardens decorated as finance and taste permit. Even modern houses in the French-built new towns retain this private aspect.

In the medinas it is possible to move from one house to another across the flat roofs, and there was a time when this was the extent of women's freedom to move around. In many villages, the houses are still built in higgledy-piggledy fashion, one against the other, with interior patios visible to the outsider only from above.

Looking into the interior courtyard of a Moroccan house.

69

THE CHANGING WORLD OF WOMEN

It is common to see female students confidently striding out in short skirts and heels, their hair cut in Western styles, and not a veil or scarf in sight.

Muslim women are often regarded by the non-Muslim world as uniformly downtrodden individuals, little more than useful chattel in a men's world. In Morocco this is not the case. Moroccan women are subject to the same constraints as women in other Muslim countries—they keep a low profile in public and their place is definitely in the home—but in the big cities at least, customs have changed considerably. Today women ride scooters, drive cars, and occasionally eat and even discreetly smoke in public.

One notable development in recent years has been the increased resources allocated to education for girls. In 1989 women represented only 40.4 percent of secondary school pupils, but their numbers are rising; in the 1990s there are more girls in secondary education. There are now several mixed-sex schools.

WOMEN'S DRESS

A women's literacy class. Women lag far behind men in education.

Although more and more women are now going out to work, many still wear a *kaftan*—a long outer garment—and a veil or at least a scarf covering their hair. Older women continue to wear the veil, perhaps more out of tradition than for any other reason, and are often seen with their jeans-clad or short-skirted daughters. Another reason for wearing traditional dress is that it protects the fashionable finery underneath. This is often the case with young and obviously emancipated women, where the slit in the side of the kaftan reveals clothes that would not be out of place in Europe.

In conservative country areas, there are a few predominantly Arab villages where the women continue to be totally enveloped in black with just one eye showing. Berber custom is different yet again. Berber women

work in the fields, and although they will modestly draw a headscarf across their faces as necessary, veils and kaftans are not as a rule part of their normal dress. This varies from region to region but is unfailingly colorful and consists of long skirts, blouses, and shawls with floral patterns, stripes, or embroidery. Hands are sometimes tinted with henna and faces tattooed.

The kaftan is the most common dress for women.

TRADITIONAL DRESS

The Moroccan version of the veil, in most cases, is a light and filmy covering for the nose, mouth, and chin. Some veils match the kaftan with which they are worn. Others are in contrasting colors.

Kaftans come in every color of the rainbow. They can be plain or patterned, and many have decorative embroidery. The best are pretty, fashionable garments and groups of women in their best kaftans can look like clusters of jewel-colored butterflies.

Men also wear a long outer garment—the djellaba. By comparison with women's kaftans they are plain in color. Most are shades of grey, brown, cream, white, or black; a few may be striped. Many men wear the djellaba as a matter of course, but others have adopted Western dress.

RELIGION

TOWARD THE END OF THE SEVENTH CENTURY A.D. Arab military missionaries, fired with a fierce desire to convert the world to Islam—the new religion founded by the Prophet Mohammed—turned their attention to the North African coastal plain. Oqba ben Nafi, one of the first of these pioneers into the wilds of Africa, led his cavalry into what is now modern Morocco around 683.

Despite his successful invasion, Oqba made little attempt to establish long-term control over Morocco. The greater part of the country still remained unconquered, but many northern Berber tribes, attracted by the energy of the new religion and its adherents, willingly converted to Islam.

In subsequent decades, more Arabs appeared on the scene, similarly bent both on conquest and on spreading Islam. Their efforts met with varying degrees of success but it was not until the arrival of Moulay Idriss in 788 that Islam was established as the religion of the majority and a measure of unity was achieved.

Moulay Idriss was welcomed in the ancient Roman city of Volubilis by already converted Berber tribesmen. With their aid he set about converting the rest. He proved so successful in this endeavor, and his power increased so dramatically, that in 791 enemies as far away as Baghdad sent murderers to poison him.

After his death, he was buried in a small town that he had founded and that bore his name. Today Moulay Idriss is the holiest town in Morocco, and until recently non-Muslims were not permitted to remain in the town overnight.

Opposite: **Inside the Fès Mosque.**

Above: **Moulay Idriss (with the green roof) is a shrine in memory of the establishment of Islam in Morocco and a memorial to Moulay Idriss, who played such a large role in this enterprise.**

ISLAM IN PRACTICE

The word "Islam" means "submission to God." The belief that lies at the very heart of this religion is that there is only one God—Allah—and that Mohammed is his prophet. The Muslim also believes that the Angel Gabriel appeared to Mohammed and dictated to him the Koran (Islam's holy book), which contains the word of God detailing how true believers should conduct their lives. The principles expressed in the Koran can be applied to almost every moment of a Muslim's existence. Islam, therefore, is not simply a religion but also a way of life.

Reading the Koran is an important part of Islamic practice.

Believing, and testifying, that there is no god but Allah, and that Mohammed is his prophet, is also the first of the five "pillars," or major observances, of Islam. The other four requirements are to pray five times a day, to observe the fast of *Ramadan* ("rah-mah-DAN"), to give at least a small proportion of one's income to help support the poor and to provide for the upkeep of mosques, and to make a pilgrimage to Mecca, the birthplace of Islam.

To remind believers of their obligations, *muezzins* ("moo-EZ-zins") chanting from the tops of minarets call people to prayer much as bells are rung in Christian churches to signal that a service is beginning. Muslims can pray wherever they wish, although a mosque is preferable, especially on Friday, which is the Islamic holy day. Friday prayers in the mosque are usually accompanied by a sermon.

Ramadan is the ninth month of the Muslim year, and for the duration of the month Muslims do not eat or drink between sunrise and sunset. The very devout sometimes deny themselves even more severely and refrain from smoking, taking medicines, and even swallowing their saliva. In Morocco the fast is particularly difficult to observe when Ramadan falls in the height of the summer heat. Sunset, however, brings relief for all Muslims wherever they are, and the evenings are filled with feasting and rejoicing. A final meal is taken just before sunrise, and the fast begins again early in the morning as soon as there is enough light to distinguish between a black thread and a white.

The pilgrimage to Mecca is required only if there is enough money available for the long journey and the expenses of the pilgrimage.

Giving alms at Fès Mosque. Setting aside a part of one's income for the relief of the poor and the upkeep of mosques is a requirement for Muslims.

BREAKING THE RAMADAN FAST

As darkness falls during Ramadan, Moroccans traditionally break their fast with a bowl of *harira* ("hah-REER-rah") soup. The basis of this soup is lamb broth enriched with diced lamb, lentils, chickpeas, onions, garlic, fresh herbs, and spices. It is frequently colored with tomatoes and thickened at the last moment with fresh yeast, flour, or beaten eggs.

The soup is often served along with tidbits such as fresh dates, dried figs, hardboiled eggs, and fried, honeyed pastries called *shebbakia* ("sherh-BAH-kee-ah").

Boys in a Koran school.

ISLAM IN MOROCCO

For some non-Muslims, Islam is synonymous with intolerance and violent fundamentalism. The average Moroccan, however, although devout and conscientious about his religious duties, is in no way a fanatic.

Geographically Morocco is remote from the center of Islam and has remained virtually untouched by the often violent conflicts between rival Muslim sects, particularly the Sunni and Shi'a sects. The development of Moroccan Islam has also been influenced by Berber religious practices that predate the arrival of the Arabs and their new religion. Finally, in more recent times, Morocco's desire to have good relationships with the West, and particularly with Europe, has brought home the value of avoiding the excesses of extremist fundamentalism as well as what outsiders might regard as brutal Islamic practices.

Morocco has adopted the Western calendar and many Western customs, such as the New Year's Day holiday. Offices and shops close on Sundays rather than on Fridays. That said, even the busiest streets in the biggest towns suddenly become quiet on Friday at midday, and large congregations flock to the mosques to pray and listen to the Friday sermon. The fact also remains that in some country areas, where few are concerned with opening and closing times or business in the Western and urban sense, Friday is still the day of rest, and souks are likely to close in the afternoon.

SAINTS, SHRINES, AND SACRED SYMBOLS

The Moroccan countryside is dotted with whitewashed, domed buildings called *koubbas* ("KOO-bah"). These are the tombs of *marabouts* ("MAH-rah-boo")—saintly men with a local cult following. In theory, Islam does not accept the idea of there being any intermediary between the individual

A marabout tomb. The cult of marabouts probably has its roots in early Berber worship focused around individual holy men.

and God. When Muslims pray, they speak directly to Allah, but Islam in Morocco is tolerant of these cults of saints and their shrines.

Koubbas are especially popular with women, who will visit the tomb of a favorite saint or maybe even a supposedly sacred tree or stream. Generally they ask for favors such as relief from an illness, or plead for intercession. Sometimes a visit is an opportunity to give vent to grief for some misfortune.

Magic and superstitious beliefs are taboo for the strictly orthodox Muslim. But old folk practices die hard, and every medina has its fortune-teller as well as shops selling magic potions and strange concoctions against evils of one kind or another.

Muslims are required to pray five times a day.

The prohibition against non-Muslims entering a mosque is not universal throughout Islam. In Morocco the rule is being slowly relaxed. Since early 1994 visitors have been permitted to enter the impressive Hassan II Mosque recently completed in Casablanca. Whether the new tolerance will eventually extend to all mosques in Morocco depends partly on local public reaction and partly on the behavior of visitors who choose to take advantage of the new regulation.

THE MOSQUE: CENTER OF RELIGIOUS LIFE

The focus of Muslim religious activity is the mosque, which in many cases has an attached *medersa* ("may-DER-sa"), or student college. The most obvious sign of the presence of a mosque is the square, often green minarets from the top of which the muezzin calls the faithful to prayer. These days, his voice is generally amplified by a loudspeaker, but his words and their message are the same.

The mosque is the meeting place for prayer and usually comprises a courtyard with a fountain and a hall for prayer with aisles segregating men from women. A niche in one of the walls indicates the direction of Mecca. This is called the *mihrab* ("MEEH-rab") and to its right there is a pulpit called a *minbar,* from which the *imam* ("ee-MAM") reads the Koran, preaches his sermons, and leads the congregation in prayer.

"Mosque" is a word meaning "the place where one bows down in prayer." Prayer within the mosque, indeed prayer anywhere within Islam, whether in a prayer hall, at home, or elsewhere, involves a fixed number of genuflections and prostrations. This ritual prostration, however, is not usually visible in Morocco because non-Muslims are not permitted to enter the mosques.

Muslims demonstrate their respect for the mosque by removing their shoes before entering its precincts. A pile of shoes beside an inconspicuous doorway is often the sign of a mosque entrance and a quick peep through the archway into the courtyard frequently reveals worshippers performing ritual ablutions—washing their hands, face, and feet, often at a central fountain.

MEDERSAS AND MINARETS

Medersas are colleges and residence halls that were once attached to the mosques and served as early universities. They also have minarets. Unlike the mosques, Morocco's fine medersas are open to all, even though a few may have prayer halls that are still in use and therefore off limits to non-Muslims.

Some of these residential colleges were built by pious sultans but many developed from domestic buildings, sometimes the houses of the principal teachers. Either way

The minaret of El Mansour mosque in Marrakech. A pair of storks nest nearby.

they alleviated the lot of impoverished (male) students from the countryside who often had to walk vast distances to places of learning. The buildings themselves were elaborately ornamented, but the students generally lived in cell-like rooms, often dark and damp and badly ventilated. Lodging, drinking water, and bread, however, were free. Similar buildings called *zaouias* ("za-OO-ee-ahs") were attached to many koubbas.

Keyhole arches around the esplanade in the Hassan II Mosque.

CASABLANCA'S HASSAN II MOSQUE

The inhabitants of Casablanca have long felt that the city lacked an architectural monument, a focus that would put it on an equal footing with the four imperial cities and complement its economic importance. This deficiency was remedied in 1993 when the Hassan II Mosque opened for worship and provided Morocco with a magnificent spiritual heart for the country's commercial center.

The new mosque is the largest mosque in Africa and second only in size to the Great Mosque in Mecca. It cost around US$750 million, which critics say Morocco could ill afford. The money was raised by voluntary, nationwide public donations, and in general the project appears to have the support of the majority of the population.

In reality, Casablanca's new landmark is considerably more than a mosque. When complete with its steam baths, its medersa, library, museum, and conference facilities, possibly by the end of the millennium, it will be an extensive Islamic center. The mosque itself opened in mid-1993. Its size and beauty have been recognized as nothing short of dazzling.

The exterior is decorated in a restful green and white—the Islamic colors for tolerance and peace. A series of sculpted marble columns and characteristically Moroccan keyhole arches enclose the central building, which stands on a vast esplanade that can accommodate 80,000 worshippers. Mosaic decorations, traditional in both color and design, cover fountains and facades, and monumental metal doors glitter in the sunshine. The prayer hall within has room for 20,000 male worshippers. They prostrate themselves on an inlaid marble floor with colors and patterns made to resemble a Moroccan carpet. Women occupy two separate mezzanines and are shielded from view by delicately carved cedarwood screens.

Light filters in through rose windows and large bay windows that look out over the Atlantic Ocean. On fine days the roof over the central court can be opened to the blue sky above. When it is closed, glittering Venetian chandeliers and hundreds of small lights set into the decorative plasterwork gently illuminate the vast expanses of the sanctuary, the gorgeously painted ceiling, the elegant calligraphy, and other Islamic motifs.

At 575 feet (172.5 m) the minaret is both the tallest structure in the country and the tallest minaret in the world. It is surmounted by a dome that adds another 120 feet (36 m), and above that an arrow that pierces three golden globes of descending size. There are plans for a laser beam, visible for 20 miles (32 km), that will point like a giant finger toward Mecca.

"[Allah's] Throne was upon the water." This quotation from the Koran inspired the choice of location for the Hassan II Mosque, which sits on a platform built out over the sea.

Minarets stand out on the skyline of Fès.

FÈS, CITY OF MINARETS

Oxford, England, is known as the city of dreaming spires. Morocco's Fès could equally be dubbed the city of minarets. Each of these characteristically slim, square towers indicates the presence of a mosque and underlines the city's role as the country's Islamic heartland.

Fès is the most ancient of Morocco's four imperial capitals. Its site—a long, flat valley enclosed by ranges of hills and bisected by a small river—was chosen in the late eighth century by Moulay Idriss I, the first Arab to establish wide-ranging and effective control in Morocco by subduing previously unconquered Berber tribes and converting them to Islam.

Within 50 years of its founding, Fès became home to two groups of Muslim refugees, the first from Cordoba in Andalusian Spain and the second from Kairouan in Tunisia. At the time these were the two most important cities in western Islam, and the commercial acumen and cultural skills the refugees brought with them had an enormous impact on the new city. Houses, shops, public baths, and flour mills were built on both sides of the river and merchants traveled from far and wide to buy and sell in the busy markets.

Two great mosques, the Karaouiyine and the Andalous, with their associated student colleges and residences, were both the main focus of the city's religious life and masterpieces of Islamic architecture of the period. At the same time, because Islamic learning centers on the Koran, these institutions developed as places not only of prayer but also of religious knowledge, in addition to the study of mathematics, philosophy, and medicine.

In 1958-59 the Karaouiyine Mosque, now acknowledged as one of the oldest universities in the world, celebrated its 11th centenary. During the Middle Ages, the university had a great reputation as a center of Islamic culture. By the 14th century, it had 8,000 students. The university still functions today but most of its faculties and students have moved to more convenient premises outside the medina. The mosque, however, still remains, as it were, the Mecca of Morocco's religious life and governs, for example, the timing of Ramadan and other Islamic festivals.

At the height of its power, at the beginning of the 13th century, Fès boasted 785 mosques for 125,000 inhabitants—roughly one mosque for every 170 people. Today a mosque is a legal requirement in each of the 187 different quartiers of Fès el Bali—the original old town—but the law is hardly necessary because the city still has no fewer than 300 mosques. It also has Morocco's most sacred saintly shrine—the *zaouia* ("za-OO-ee-ah") erected in memory of Moulay Idriss II. By all accounts he was not a particularly saintly man but is revered as the effective founder of Fès (he completed what his father had started) and as the son of the founder of the Arab Moroccan state.

Fès is three cities in one. In the 13th century, when old Fès was bulging to capacity within its walls, New Fès— Fès el Djedid ("je-DEED")—was built close by on slightly higher ground. It is a totally different city, characterized by wide open spaces, splendid palaces, and military and administrative buildings. In the 20th century the French built a new town some distance outside the two ancient Fès cities.

LANGUAGE

ARABIC IS MOROCCO'S OFFICIAL but not its only language. An individual Moroccan, for example, may well have Berber, Arab, Spanish, Negro, and Jewish blood. The country's languages reflect this heritage.

The vast majority of Moroccans are Arabized Berbers, that is, Muslim Berbers who have been strongly influenced by Arab culture and lifestyle. Around two-thirds of the population have Arabic as their first language and speak varying amounts of one of the local Berber languages. Among the Berbers who live in remote areas, Berber is the language of their daily life.

The presence of the French during the Protectorate period also means that French has a high profile as a second language. Official and administrative documents are drafted in both Arabic and French. Identity cards, for example, are in Arabic on one side and French on the other.

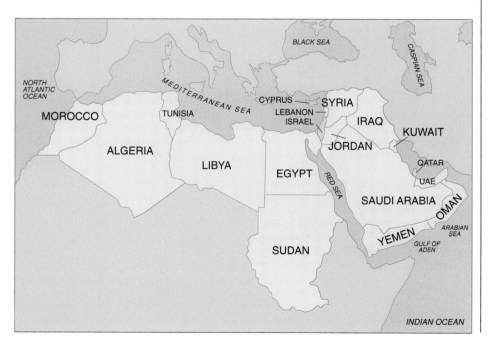

Opposite: **Men at a grain market. Business is widely conducted in French.**

Left: **Countries where Arabic is the official language. It is estimated that about 60 million people from the countries of North Africa in the west, across most of the Arabian peninsula and as far east as Syria and Iraq have Arabic as their mother tongue. A much larger number—around 150 million—understand, read, or write it insofar as it is their language of trade or the language of their religion. The Koran—Islam's equivalent of the Bible—is written in Arabic and recited in Arabic by all Muslims.**

ARABIC MOROCCAN STYLE

Modern written Arabic is by and large the language of the Koran modified for use in modern times, so it is the same all over the world.

Written Arabic is the same for all Arabic speakers across the world. The spoken language, however, differs from country to country. The Arabic dialect spoken in Morocco is known as Maghrebi Arabic.

In countries that are far apart, the differences can be enormous and individual dialects mutually unintelligible. For instance, an Iraqi finds it difficult to communicate with a Moroccan, but since the Moroccan dialect is similar to that of Algeria and Tunisia, inhabitants of these three neighboring countries can generally understand each other.

One of the problems resulting from the numerous different dialects of Arabic is that any one word may be pronounced in many different ways. As a consequence, phonetic spellings or transliterations of Arabic words vary. A case in point is *b'stilla* ("bis-TEEL-ya")—Morocco's famous pigeon pie—which is found as *pasteeya, bisteeya, bstila, pastilla, pastela,* and *bastela*. Nevertheless, there are a number of phrases that are understood wherever they are used across the entire Arabic-speaking world. These include *Insha'Allah* ("in-SHAH-lah") or "God willing," and the formal greeting *Salaam oualeikum* ("sa-LAAM wa-LAY-koom"), meaning "Peace be with you."

BERBER LANGUAGES

There is no one standard Berber language but rather a group of languages spoken by separate Berber communities in various parts of northern Africa. Moroccan Berbers speak one of three languages. Riffian is common among the inhabitants of the Rif mountains in the north and parts of the Middle Atlas range. Other Middle Atlas tribes speak Braber, as do some High Atlas dwellers, while the language of other parts of the High Atlas, the southernmost valleys, and the Anti-Atlas, is Chleuh. For Chleuh speakers, Riffian is virtually a foreign language. Braber lies somewhere between the two.

Since there is no standard Berber language, no universally accepted Berber script has evolved. There was a time when a few individual Berber languages were written in their own ancient script, as in the case of the Tuareg tribes in the Sahara Desert, but except for a few inscriptions, the Berber languages have practically no written literature. Today Arabic script is used for writing all the surviving Berber languages.

In Morocco, monolingual Berber speakers are now in a minority. Most Berbers, except the most isolated, can understand some Arabic and for written communication among themselves use the Arabic script.

Many English words have Arabic origins. Among the best-known are:
cipher
algebra
arsenal
admiral
alcove
alkali
alcohol
lemon
sugar
coffee

OTHER LANGUAGES

With the exception of the very young and the very isolated, most Moroccans speak at least a smattering of French. This is a legacy of the Protectorate period, when French was established as the language of learning. The language is taught, even today, in the tiniest schools in the loneliest locations. The best educated are fluent French speakers.

The evidence of previous French presence in Morocco is visible, and audible, at every turn. The months of the year are *janvier, fevrier, mars,* and so on, as in French, and traffic direction signs are invariably in both Arabic and French. Street names, especially in the cities, are frequently in both languages. French is also the language of business, and this enables Morocco to communicate easily with the outside world, and particularly with European countries, which are Morocco's major trading partners.

Arabic script lends itself to decorative uses.

Following Moroccan independence, Spanish has not fared as well as French. Many inhabitants of the old Spanish Zone in the north—the rugged Rif mountain range and the narrow strip along the Mediterranean coast as far as the Algerian border—still speak Spanish, but their numbers are dwindling. French is now the main second language in this once Spanish-dominated part of the country. Meanwhile English has been introduced as a second foreign language in secondary schools and at higher education levels. The purpose is to facilitate participation in international trade, which is increasingly in English, and to improve communication with English-speaking tourists, whose presence is becoming an ever more important part of the Moroccan economy.

THE MEDIA

Moroccans have the choice of eight Arabic language daily newspapers, in addition to five others published in French. There are also numerous periodicals in Arabic that deal with economic and political events. For a country with a small readership—literacy levels are still low—this is a remarkable amount of choice. In effect, however, independent comment is not as wide-ranging as one would expect, because the most important publications voice the government or establishment point of view or are linked to particular political parties.

The most important daily newspapers are the Arabic language *Al-Anba'a,* meaning "Information," and *Maroc Soir* and *Le Matin du Sahara,* which are both in French. These publications tend to support the establishment.

Similarly, radio and television are both generally state-controlled, but because they reach a far wider audience, they are of much greater importance than the press. In 1990 UNESCO estimated that there were around 5,250,000 radios in Morocco—about one for every four people and therefore probably more than one per household, since families tend to be large. A television set is much more expensive. Access to television is therefore more limited, but the number of people, especially in urban areas, who own sets is growing rapidly. A set in a small hotel, a cafe, restaurant, or shop frequently draws a large audience.

Morocco has nine regional radio stations broadcasting in Arabic, French, and Berber. A nationwide TV network begun in 1962 broadcasts in French and Arabic and carries commercial advertising. A second channel has recently become available on a subscription basis. The main Spanish TV channels can also be received in Morocco.

ARTS

THE LABYRINTHINE MAZES of the medinas enclose unique architectural jewels, and Morocco has a vital heritage of arts and crafts that are gaining international recognition. Moroccans also have a rich tradition of music and dance. Their classical music draws on Andalusian and Arab sources and includes religious music totally different in character from the religious music of the Christian world. Popular music in Morocco has borrowed modern instruments and themes from the West but continues to derive most of its inspiration from closer to home. Finally, since independence, artists have begun to develop arts such as drama, sculpture, and painting.

The country's arts amd crafts and architecture are extremely important from the point of view of the economy. Moroccans are beginning to realize the importance of their architectural heritage and to take steps to prevent vulnerable buildings from collapse.

The production of handcrafted items employs over seven percent of Morocco's workforce and generates substantial foreign exchange earnings.

Opposite: **The production of handicrafts employs over seven percent of the work force.**

Left: **Pottery is a Moroccan specialty.**

ARCHITECTURE—THE ARAB LEGACY

The Arabs who brought Islam to Morocco and converted the indigenous Berbers to their new religion also introduced a wealth of ideas about architecture and methods of decoration. As the centuries went by, successive sultans, both Berber and Arab, constructed mosques, medersas, minarets, and other buildings connected with the practice of their religion, as well as palaces and public buildings to reflect their temporal power.

Architectural achievements in Morocco, however, were not mere copies of glories to be found elsewhere. The vast forests of oak, pine, and cedar allowed local artisans to develop a tradition of decorative woodcarving, and the absence of abundant supplies of precious metals led them to apply their creative skills to stucco and ceramic mosaic.

Both of these materials and the techniques for using them were Eastern in origin but were perfected in Andalusian Spain. They came to Morocco by way of Moorish refugees from the Christian reconquest of the country. The refugees also brought with them the tradition of domes, pillars, and semicircular and horseshoe arches.

Moroccan mosques took as their inspiration the great mosques of Kairouan in Tunisia and Cordoba in Spain. They are unadorned on the outside and their roofs are covered in plain green tiles. But in contrast to the austere simplicity of the exterior the entrance is a highly decorated door that leads into paved courtyards where fountains play and walls

Bahia Palace in Marrakech. The wealthy built themselves personal oases filled with beauty and hidden away from the heat, dust, and hubbub of the outside world.

THE WRITING ON THE WALL

The Islamic religion discourages pictorial representation of living things and prohibits any representation of God. This is one of the reasons why the Arabic script has been raised to the level of an art form.

Arabic writing is quintessentially elegant and offers enormous scope for imaginative presentation in rectangular, circular, and oblong shapes and in the forms of fruit and birds, buildings and stars, lamps, and a host of other configurations. It also lends itself to use on a wide variety of materials from paper and stone to stucco, ceramic, glass, wood, metal, ivory, and fabric. Within a religious building, it is most often used for naming Allah and his attributes and for the decorative presentation of verses of the Koran.

The words that appear most frequently in the Arabic script used as decoration are those of the Bismillah *("bihs-mih-LAH")— "Bismillahir Rahmanir Rahim" —"In the Name of Allah, the Compassionate, the Merciful," which is the opening phrase of every chapter of the Koran.*

are covered with green, blue, red, and black mosaics and expanses of exquisitely patterned stucco. Doors, window frames, and screens were carved in patterns so delicate that they look like lace, and frieze after frieze carries calligraphic inscriptions and bands of intertwined foliage and flowers and geometric patterns. Towering above all this grace is the square minaret so characteristic of the Maghreb countries.

Palaces and other major buildings also feature the same lively and open feeling of Islamic styles with their emphasis on space.

PROTECTING ONESELF

In the south in particular, tribal warfare and the struggles of emerging dynasties produced architecture with defense as its prime objective. This ranged from tall, crenellated, fortified houses and villages to cities encircled by massive walls pierced by gates of monumental proportions.

In the countryside and desert areas, construction materials were rudimentary and of poor quality—crudely made unfired bricks and plaster—but the buildings were often adorned with geometric decorations carved into the mud or onto the rough wood of the doors. This decorative tradition, however simple, has continued to the present, although the doors are now metal and paint is widely available. Windows too were and still are carefully embellished with ornamentation ranging from crude daubings to the pretty wrought-iron grilles inspired by Moorish Spain. At the same time, much of the decoration in areas close to the Sahara reveal Morocco's contacts with the totally different world of Black Africa.

The ramparts of the kasbah in Rabat show crenellated walls with a large bab, or gate.

The great walled cities, for their part, were intended not only to defend a tribe or a dynasty but also to reflect their builder's wealth, success, and power. This was sometimes short-lived, especially when succeeding incoming dynasties and rivals destroyed what previous sultans had constructed.

The city walls were high, crenelated, thick, and usually plain, but their huge *babs*, or gateways, were an opportunity for sumptuous decoration and the ostentatious display of wealth. They were generally built of stone and had a central archway, sometimes flanked by crenelated towers.

BAB EL MANSOUR

The Bab el Mansour in Meknes is the finest of Morocco's collection of city gates. It is immense, perfectly proportioned, and richly decorated with green and white ceramic. The central bay, where the gateway itself is set, is flanked by squat bastions similarly decorated and partly supported by elegant marble columns. The decoration is based on a traditional pattern called *darj w ktarf,* meaning "cheek and shoulder." The mosaic work is elaborate and richly colored. There are also layers of cutaway black tiles, and the ornamental inscriptions surmounting the whole include the claim that there is no gate in the Islamic world of the 17th century that can be called its equal.

RELAXATION IN PEACE

Another of the many artistic ideas that Morocco gleaned from its connections with Spain was that of the formal but restful garden with its greenery, fountains, and running water. These gardens are quiet havens where women come to visit each other while their children play. Park benches are filled with students deep in study, while members of the older generation skim through the newspaper or snooze in the sun.

The capital, Rabat, has a delightful walled Andalusian Garden. It was constructed by the French in the first half of the 20th century but is called Andalusian because its design is so faithful to the ancient Spanish garden tradition. Beds of hibiscus and roses, lilies, marigolds, poinsettias, and sweet-smelling herbs are separated by straight paths and, as in all of Morocco's parks, the garden is filled with strollers.

Many cities today have shady parks where the air is filled with the scent of orange blossoms, and the lilac flowers of the jacarandas vie with the blue of the north African sky.

CARPETS, KILIMS, AND SILVER

Traditional handicrafts include rugs, carpets, metalwork, jewelry, leather goods, woodwork, and pottery. Of these, the most important are Morocco's colorful knotted carpets and woven rugs. Carpets from Rabat are generally acknowledged as the finest and most valuable. Their design—a central medallion and a wide border with an intricate pattern—is Turkish in origin and was introduced in the 18th century.

Rugs are an important handicraft in Morocco.

The woven *kilims,* or rugs, made by various Berber tribes are quite different, and designs are passed from one generation to the next. It is claimed that a glance at the pattern and the colors used will reveal at least the region, possibly the tribe, and in some cases the individual family that produced the rug.

Middle Atlas kilims are mostly worked in beiges and browns. In the High Atlas reds and ochres predominate, whereas in the area around Ouarzazate reds and blues figure prominently. Some rugs are finely worked in a combination of wool and silk: many are quite thin and the best are hung in tents or on the wall rather than put on the floor.

Metalwork similarly ranges from the simple and utilitarian to the delicate and decorative. The metalworking souks reverberate to the beating of copper and brass and to the gentle tap of the jeweler's hammer. Artisans transform silver into incised teapots and trays, daggers and

JEWELRY FOR ALL OCCASIONS

Whatever their means or status, Moroccan women wear jewelry as a matter of course. A countrywoman bent double under a load of firewood may well be wearing a heavy silver chain decorated with old coins or a necklace of chunky amber beads. Her more sophisticated sister in town may choose a more contemporary style, but nonetheless she is likely to be adorned at least with a necklace, ring, and earrings, and possibly with bracelets and pins as well.

In some cases, decoration goes beyond mere adornment. Tattoos on the hands or faces of some Berber women are intended to ward off illness or misfortune. Silver "hands of Fatima" (Fatima was the Prophet Mohammed's daughter) are worn as pendants and for the same purpose. Rather different are certain large bracelets with protruding knobs that, so the story goes, could be used by their wearers in self-defense.

scabbards, Koran boxes with intricate silver-wire decorations, and above all the bracelets, necklaces, pins, and pendants with which Moroccan women love to adorn themselves.

Morocco's abundant sheep and goats provide a source of skins for the leather trade, and "bound in Morocco" has long been a phrase used to indicate the good quality of a book's binding. Moroccan leather has also been used for centuries to make sandals and saddlebags, and especially the distinctive pointed slippers known as *babouches* ("bah-BOOSH") that are worn in various forms by most Moroccan men and many Moroccan women.

Woodworking is another Moroccan craft that has survived the march of mechanized progress. Local woodworkers produce a variety of items from simple, utilitarian dishes and boxes to painted and carved chairs and tables. Some of their handiwork is painstakingly inlaid with contrasting veneers or mother-of-pearl.

Musicians performing in the Djemm el'Fna in Marrakech.

The day is punctuated by the call of the muezzin reminding Moslems of their obligation to pray. His chanting voice, tinnily amplified, rings out from a loudspeaker on the minaret that towers above streets and homes.

MUSIC IN THE AIR

The most widely heard modern music is *chabbi*, which means "popular." It is often played in cafés, many of which keep instruments specifically for the musicians who come to sip a glass of tea and then launch into a jam session. Chabbi began as music performed by traveling entertainers who collected and composed songs as they went along. In recent times, it is no longer confined to impromptu performances in public squares. The best groups now perform regularly on radio and television.

This kind of music is a mixture of Arab, African, and Western styles. It also includes elements from traditional Berber music, sung Arabic poetry, and ritual religious music, and is played by musicians who work together like a Western group. At the end of a song, however, an instrumental section is sometimes played at double speed so that the audience bursts into shouting, dancing, and syncopated clapping.

Another form of modern music called *rai* (rye)—also rock-style and backed by electric instruments—has lyrics that focus on such topics as sex, alcohol, drugs, and cars, and is not popular in conservative parts of Moroccan society.

COUNTRY STYLE

Among the Berber tribes, especially where the illiteracy rate is high, music and dancing play an important role in community life because they are often the strongest form of self-expression. Some forms of Berber music involve the whole village in circular dances and a kind of chanted singing. The women hold hands and move in slow circles around the drummers, who crouch close to the flames of a glowing fire that tightens the skins on the drums. It is rhythmic, compelling music and is usually performed on a festive occasion or in honor of visitors or guests.

The Berbers also have special ritual music for important lifetime events such as a marriage, or for an exorcism or purification ceremony. And in days not so long ago the majority of rural people received information about events outside their immediate circle from professional musicians who traveled from village to village singing the news. These *imdyazn* ("IM-dee-AZN"), as they were called, have now largely been put out of business by the advent of radio and television.

A performance of a traditional dance.

Morocco's equivalent of the classical music of the West developed from songs and music introduced by Arabs from the East and refugees from Andalusia. It is generally played by one of the country's three most important orchestras, which are based in Fès, Meknes, and Tangier—the cities most profoundly influenced by Moorish Spain.

LEISURE

LEISURE PURSUITS in Morocco are a mixture of simple and traditional entertainments for the majority, with a few sophisticated and more expensive activities for the better off. Some of the latter activities are Moroccan in origin, but others were introduced by foreigners during the Protectorate period. In addition, certain sports are being actively developed because of their potential for attracting tourists.

The way people spend their leisure time depends on where they live, their position in society, and their economic circumstances. The poor often do not have a lot of spare time to occupy, although in farming and nomadic communities there may be periods of intense activity followed by periods with little to do. But if you live far from civilization, if your home lacks a basic amenity such as electricity, or you cannot read, then most of your leisure is probably occupied by chatting with your neighbors, playing simple traditional games, or listening to the radio. On special occasions—holidays or the arrival of a friend or a visitor—there may be celebrations with music and dancing.

Town and city dwellers, especially those who are financially better off, have more choices. These could include a visit to the cinema or a swimming pool—municipal pools are quite common—or an afternoon at a soccer match, this being the national sport. Other possibilities are a visit to the beach for those who live near the coast or watching television if one is available. Men often take advantage of the television sets that flicker in the corner of so many cafés.

For a few there is golf, hunting, shooting, and fishing, and water sports are being developed at many resorts.

Opposite: **Chatting in a café is a popular leisure activity for men.**

Below: **Cinemas are mostly for men. Popular fare includes Indian films and adventure movies.**

ENTERTAINMENT MOROCCAN STYLE

For Moroccans, a great deal of leisure is genuinely leisurely in nature. Living life to the full does not necessarily mean cramming some activity into every spare moment, and a great deal of leisure is family-oriented in one way or another. Eating out is not common, but eating well is much enjoyed. Most people place great store in eating good food at home in the convivial presence of family and friends and welcome an excuse for a *diffa*, or banquet, however simple it may be.

A family resting during a leisurely promenade.

Similarly, families go out together. The evening promenade is especially popular during the heat of summer. In big cities smartly dressed strollers frequent the cafés on the shady boulevards and watch the world go by. In less sophisticated places, women and children enjoy an excursion to a park or some other cool spot, while many men tend to congregate in cafés to discuss local affairs and exchange gossip over coffee or glasses of mint tea. Some may smoke a little kif, or hashish, usually upstairs or somewhere out of sight. The practice is not encouraged, but it is hard to eradicate.

Evening is the time for window-shopping. In the medinas, the shutters are removed after the afternoon siesta, the streets come alive, and the markets buzz with activity.

TRADITIONAL ENTERTAINMENT

Part of the fun of the evening promenade is the chance of seeing any one of dozens of different kinds of itinerant entertainers. These include storytellers and magicians, acrobats, jugglers and dancers, musicians and singers, snake charmers with mesmerized and mesmerizing reptiles, and tame monkeys taught to perform tricks.

The Djemm el'Fna in Marrakech, in particular, is famed for its congregation of traditional entertainers who appear at dusk. Crowds drift from one group or stall to another, and there is continuous pulsating activity. Storytellers attract large circles of listeners. Tumblers, acrobats, and skillful jugglers weave their way through the audience as it ebbs and flows. Gaudily dressed watersellers festooned with brass cups ring their bells insistently, adding to the din of singers, the blare of pop music, musicians playing reed pipes, and drummers beating out wild rhythms, some of which can induce trance.

Special outings usually take the form of a trip to a *moussem* ("MOO-sem"), a festival in honor of a local saint. These are enormously joyful occasions with a country-fair atmosphere.

A visit to a hammam, *or public steam bath, can be a necessity for those who do not have running (not to mention hot) water in their homes. For others it may be primarily a social occasion. Every medina has its hammam with plentiful supplies of hot water and sometimes opportunities for an invigorating massage. Bathing is strictly segregated, and modesty is important. Both men and women wear swimsuits. Sometimes different periods are reserved for men and women; occasionally there are separate rooms.*

Boys playing soccer. Budding strikers practice in the streets, on the beaches, and on empty lots, and televised matches draw large audiences.

THE SPORTING LIFE

The national sport is soccer, but there is increasing interest in a range of other sports such as tennis and swimming. To some extent this new interest is driven by economic concerns. Tourism is one of Morocco's biggest hard-currency earners. Morocco can offer sports-minded visitors golf, water sports, hunting, shooting, fishing, and adventure vacations, while the influx of visitors boosts employment in many depressed areas.

Farmers, for example, and others living in places where the scenery is dramatic and exotic benefit from the demand for open-air vacations. On the coasts, vast stretches of beach in generally unproductive areas are being developed as seaside resorts.

SOCCER FOR ALL

In 1986, Morocco gained a place in the World Cup quarter finals. Although their success story came to an end at this point, team members were feted on their return home, loaded with valuable rewards for their efforts—villas, cars, and business enterprises—and treated to a grand victory parade through Casablanca. Sadly for enthusiasts, the national team was much less successful in 1990 and failed to qualify for the championships.

GOLFING THE ROYAL WAY

Although soccer is the national obsession, golf has a longer history in Morocco. The first course opened in Tangier in 1917 and was primarily used by the diplomatic community in the international zone, as it then was. Nevertheless, several more courses, mostly in the central areas and main cities, opened even before independence.

Since the accession of King Hassan II, who is an avid golfer, the sport has increased in popularity. It is significant that the word "Royal" features in the name of many clubs. The 1980s and 1990s have seen courses increase in number and dramatically improve in quality. This has a lot to do with royal patronage and the realization that golf can play a prominent role in attracting the kind of wealthy tourist that the country seeks. It is hoped that the prospect of perfect playing weather nearly all year round, good courses and facilities, and reasonable greens and caddy fees will prove irresistible attractions for dedicated golfers.

Morocco's best soccer teams are FAR, which is drawn from armed forces personnel, WIDAD and RAJA, which are both Casablanca-based, MAS from Fès, and KAC from Kénitra.

OTHER SPORTS

Golf is undeniably a game for the elite, but ordinary Moroccans have access to public swimming pools, and the country's long coastline provides ample opportunity to enjoy other water sports, such as windsurfing, sailing, and diving. At present, these are expensive in Moroccan terms, but they will slowly become accessible to a larger proportion of the population.

Another sport with an expensive image is skiing, but a number of ski resorts have operated in the Atlas mountains for several years and are well patronized by local enthusiasts in the closest towns—Fès, Meknes, and Rabat—and by youth clubs and schools. Slopes and lodge facilities do not compare in quality with those in the United States or Europe, but cross-country skiing has great potential.

FESTIVALS

MOROCCO HAS A PLETHORA OF FESTIVALS and holidays. Some are celebrated on a national scale, and many are regional or local occasions. Four major festivals are directly connected with important religious events or dates. In addition, there are a myriad of moussems, which are primarily festivals connected with the cult of a local saint or holy man.

Regardless of whether they are secular or religious in character, Moroccan festivals are joyous affairs, marked by music, dancing, feasting, and a good deal of commercial activity as well. The newer state holidays also tend to have parades and official ceremonies.

Most of the secular holidays have come into being since the country became an independent state, in the modern sense of the word, in 1956. The most important of them is the Festival of the Throne—the anniversary of the accession of King Hassan II in 1961. It is sometimes called Throne Day and is marked countrywide by fireworks, parades, music, and dancing often lasting considerably longer than one day. Green March Remembrance Day commemorates the march into the Western Sahara in 1975.

Opposite: **A young girl in her best attire at festival time.**

The fixed official state holidays are:

January 1	New Year's Day
March 3	Festival of the Throne
May 1	Labor Day
August 14	Allegiance Day
August 20	Revolution of the King and the People
November 6	Green March Remembrance Day
November 18	Independence Day

RELIGIOUS CELEBRATIONS AND HOLIDAYS

A sheep for Aïd el Kebir. The animals are bought well in advance so that they can be fattened up. They are tethered wherever there is space, often on the flat roofs of the houses.

Morocco's major religious holidays—*Aïd es Seghir* ("ah-EED es-say-GEER"), *Aïd el Kebir* ("ah-EED el-kay-BEER"), *Muharram* ("mo-HAH-ram"), and *Mouloud* ("moo-LOOD")—have long histories going back to the time when Islam was introduced. They fall on different dates each year because they are linked to the Muslim lunar calendar rather than the Gregorian solar calendar.

Aïd es Seghir is the celebration that marks the end of Ramadan, the fasting month similar in concept to the Christian Lent. The festival effectively brings Morocco to a standstill for two days, although feasting and rejoicing often continue for up to a week. Special food is prepared well in advance, and new clothes are bought for the occasion.

Aïd el Kebir commemorates Abraham's willingness to sacrifice his son, Isaac, if God so commanded. Like Aïd es Seghir, it is traditionally a family gathering. For Aïd el Kebir, every household that can afford to do so slaughters a sheep. After the feast the skins can be seen being cured in the streets.

The first day of the month of Muharram is a one-day festival to mark the Muslim New Year, but festivities for Mouloud—the birthday of the Prophet Mohammed—extend over two days. A large number of moussems also occur in the weeks before and after Mohammed's birthday.

A celebration for Aïd el Kebir, the holiday when Muslims make the pilgrimage to Mecca.

THE MUSLIM CALENDAR

The Muslim calendar is a lunar system consisting of 12 months, each starting at the new moon. Alternate months have 29 or 30 days except the last, *Dhu al-Hijjah* ("DOO al-HEE-jah"), the length of which varies over a 30-year period to keep the calendar in step with the phases of the moon. For 11 years of the cycle this month has 30 days, and the following year it has 29.

A Muslim year therefore numbers 354 or 355 days and is about 11 days shorter than the solar year. It is for this reason that the dates of the religious festivals vary. For example, in 1988, Aïd es Seghir was celebrated on May 16, whereas six years later, in 1994, it fell on March 12, and in 1995 it will probably take place on March 1. This lack of certainty occurs because the actual date is determined by the sighting of the new moon.

Years are reckoned from A.D. 622—the date of the Hegira, when opposition to his radical new ideas forced Mohammed to flee from his home in Mecca. Because the lunar year of the Muslim calendar is shorter than the solar year of the Gregorian calendar, the two systems never coincide exactly, and thus 1995 corresponds to 1415-1416 A.H. (meaning "after the Hegira") while 1996 is 1416-1417 A.H.

Ramadan is a time for self-denial mixed with restrained celebration. In the daytime Moroccans abstain from all food and drink but at sunset there is a sense of happy relief as everyone hurries home to satisfy their hunger and slake their thirst. The evenings and nights are spent in joyful feasting and relaxation before the fast begins as daylight reappears.

While singing, dancing, and general merrymaking are the order of the day, if conditions and cost permit, the highlight of moussem celebrations will be a dramatic fantasia. Horsemen brandishing rifles gallop at full speed across an open space, firing their weapons into the air as they go. The horses and their nobly dressed riders dash past, and the air is filled with swirling dust and sand, whoops, shouts, gunfire, and contagious excitement.

MOUSSEM MERRYMAKING

Moussems are primarily local events. They vary widely in their form, purpose, and style, and are the staples of festive life in rural areas.

There are an enormous number of moussems. A few have developed into substantial occasions, and one or two have become tourist attractions. Some are little more than once-a-year markets with tenuous religious connections, whereas others are harvest festivals.

The dates of individual moussems vary from year to year for two main reasons. Harvest festivals depend on the weather and the harvest being complete, whereas religious moussems are linked to the lunar calendar. Thus their dates move, just as the dates of Aïd es Seghir and other Muslim festivals move each year.

Ostensibly, the main purpose of a moussem is to honor a local marabout, or holy man, generally in the immediate surroundings of his tomb or koubba. These are usually small, white, domed buildings that can be seen dotted all over the countryside or, in cramped towns and cities, set in between ordinary shops and houses. People come to the tomb in the hope of obtaining the marabout's blessing, to ask a favor or, in the case of harvest festivals, to give thanks for what Allah has provided.

THE MAJOR MOUSSEMS

Some moussems have grown so large that the traditional focus—devotion to the marabout—has become obscured. The greatest and grandest of the moussems, and one regularly attended by the king, is held in honor of Moulay Idriss at Meknès. However, despite much holiday-type activity, it is still an intensely religious event. Conversely, at Imilchil in the eastern High Atlas mountains, the "marriage" moussem—sometimes known as the "Brides Festival"—is like a county show or state fair and is fast becoming a tourist event.

Families and communities from remote areas ride to a moussem on their donkeys.

Families travel from far and wide to attend. Buses may bring groups, but individual families and small communities from remote spots come on foot or ride in on their donkeys or mules. Tents are pitched, carpets laid on the ground, vegetables and produce set out, and the festivities get under way.

Every moussem has a strong social dimension. The gatherings are also extremely colorful events. Most rural people, particularly the women, still wear their local costume. A moussem is an opportunity to dress up in one's best clothes and put on one's finest jewelry. More important from a social point of view, perhaps, is that family members and relatives scattered into different villages can reunite, and marriages can be arranged. Politics and family matters are also discussed, information about developments and prices gets passed around, and the community dances, sings, eats, and prays together.

FOOD

MOROCCO'S FOOD IS EXOTIC, rich in its variety, and until recent times virtually unknown in the outside world. The development of what is now recognized as a unique cuisine has been made possible by the availability of a wealth of good ingredients and food traditions introduced by successive waves of invaders from the north and south and, most importantly, from the east.

Today the agricultural areas of Morocco produce numerous fruits and vegetables: oranges, lemons, pomegranates, melons, tomatoes, sweet and hot peppers, edible gourds, potatoes, almonds, olives, and figs. Fish and seafood abound on the coast, while climate and pasture in many areas enable flocks of sheep and goats to thrive. Even the desert supplies a rich harvest of dates from its remote oases.

Some of these items have always been available in Morocco and were used by the indigenous Berbers in the preparation of long-simmered stews of lamb, poultry, and vegetables and other traditional dishes. Various invaders introduced a number of now traditional ingredients, along with previously unknown preparation and cooking methods.

The Arabs introduced spices and various types of bread and dishes based on grain products, as well as delicious pastries. Meanwhile, contact with the sophisticated society of Andalusia in southern Spain taught Moroccan cooks to experiment with olives and olive oil, and combinations of fruits, nuts, and herbs in cooked dishes. In modern times, the French and even the British have also made their contributions.

Below: **The Phoenicians brought exotic spices to Morocco, as did traders from Senegal traveling from the south across the Sahara, and Arabs from the Middle East. Today no town is without its spice shop and no market lacks a stall dedicated to the sale of cinnamon, saffron, cumin, and numerous other spices.**

Opposite: **Olives are a favorite Moroccan food.**

STAPLES: BREAD AND TAJINE

Flat, round, chewy bread, freshly baked every day, is very much the staff of life. Folklore stories and various sayings underline its value and the almost religious significance with which it is regarded. For many poor people, bread combined with a few olives or dates, or perhaps a small piece of cheese, and washed down with a a glass of hot mint tea, is a meal in itself.

Tajine in a restaurant. Sizes of tajine pots vary from small dishes for one person to dishes of mammoth proportions that can hold enough food for perhaps 20 people.

Bread is eaten at every meal. It is cut in wedges and used both as an accompaniment to whatever food is being served and as a kind of fork or spoon. Crusty chunks are particularly useful for scooping up meat and vegetables, and for mopping up the tasty sauces of Morocco's many *tajine* ("ta-JEEN") stews. These are casseroles of meat and poultry named after the cooking pot in which they are cooked. Tajine pots are generally made from earthenware and are used on charcoal braziers. They consist of a flat dish with a rim and a conical lid that fits into the dish.

The most common tajine recipes are based on lamb or chicken cut into segments and marinated in olive oil with chopped onion and garlic. Various combinations of saffron, cumin, and crushed red pepper, in addition to fresh coriander and parsley, are added to give extra flavor. The meat is first sautéed and then simmered in the marinade until it is tender.

Depending on the recipe, the meat may be combined with prunes or almonds, tomatoes, vegetables, and hard-boiled eggs. A distinctive dish combines chicken, olives, and salted lemons. In cases where meat is not available, or is too expensive, tajines are made from vegetables alone.

THE NATIONAL DISH

Although a Moroccan family may eat several tajines every week, the title of national dish goes to couscous—cream-colored grains of semolina steamed over a highly-flavored stock made from meat and vegetables, and served with the meat and a sauce made from the bouillon.

Like tajine, couscous has two meanings. The word refers to the semolina itself and to the cooked dish. No one knows exactly where the name comes from, but one amusing suggestion is that it is an attempt to imitate the hissing sound that occurs when steam is forced through the holes in the steamer—the couscoussier—in which the grains are cooked.

The dish is so popular that one could say there are as many types of couscous as there are cooks. Some make a simple dish with vegetables and chickpeas. Others make it with meat, lamb, or chicken, sometimes rabbit or pigeon.

There are couscous dishes with dates and raisins, highly seasoned varieties, and plain varieties served with a spicy red pepper sauce.

OLIVES AND LEMONS

A variety of olives, and lemons pickled in lemon juice and salt, are essential ingredients in many dishes. The lemons are sold loose or packed in jars. The preserving gives the skins a silken texture and a unique flavor.

Olives come in a variety of flavors, colors, and sizes. Some stalls sell nothing but olives: bitter, unripe green olives, riper olives ranging from tan and russet through violet, and fully ripe, cured black olives.

A food vendor in the Djemm el'Fna in Marrakech.

B'STILLA

In times of rejoicing, Moroccans are likely to celebrate with a banquet featuring one of their most famous dishes—*b'stilla*.

B'stilla is usually presented as a spectacular first course. It is made with an extravagant combination of highly spiced pigeon meat, creamy lemon-flavored eggs or hard-boiled eggs, and almonds. This is baked or fried in a circular case of overlapping leaves of thin pastry and topped with a lattice-like sugar and cinnamon decoration before serving.

The pastry, known as *warka* ("WAH-kar"), is a Moroccan version of the French *mille-feuille* ("MEAL-fe-ye") pastry. The best warka is tissue-thin and so time-consuming to make that many Moroccans buy their supplies from Sudanese women who specialize in preparing it.

There are many regional versions of this dish. The classic b'stilla is said to come from Fès. Tétouan has a chicken-based version, and people living in the Middle Atlas mountains sometimes use minced beef or lamb in place of pigeon. As with couscous, b'stilla can be sweet as well as spicy, and in the capital, Rabat, b'stilla filled with rice cooked in almond milk and scented with orange-flower water is served both as a first course and as a dessert. Similarly, the inhabitants of Marrakech have developed *keneffa* ("ken-EFF-ah")—a type of b'stilla with an orange-flavored custard filling.

BARBECUED WHOLE LAMB

If circumstances permit, b'stilla may be followed by *mechoui* ("mesh-SHOE-ee")—charcoal roasted whole lamb, a Berber specialty. Lamb is the mainstay of Moroccan meat cooking. It is grilled as brochettes, minced for use as a stuffing for vegetables, and is one of the main ingredients in countless tajines and couscous recipes.

A lamb for mechoui is rubbed with garlic and spices and then cooked slowly on a spit over burning charcoal embers. It is basted regularly with herbal butter so that it becomes crisp on the outside and succulent underneath. The best mechoui is so tender that the crispy fat on the outside peels away easily and the meat comes away in the hand. The roast meat is served with spices and plain bread.

CELEBRATING AÏD EL KEBIR

Mechoui is traditionally eaten during the Aïd el Kebir festival that takes place soon after the end of Ramadan. The festival commemorates Abraham's willingness to sacrifice his son, Isaac, in obedience to God's command. At the last moment, as Abraham prepared to kill Isaac, God provided a ram as a sacrifice in place of the child.

Those who cannot afford a whole lamb for mechoui for this celebration, or who do not have the necessary large oven or spit for roasting out of doors make do with a part of a lamb. The poorest sometimes substitute roasted kid or maybe chicken.

GAZELLES' HORNS AND COILED SERPENTS

Moroccans are notorious for their love of sweet cakes, pastries, and rich dessert dishes. Pastry shops are filled with goodies based on pounded almonds, dates, and figs, flavored with the distilled essences of orange blossom or rose petals, and soaked in honey. Little "lovers' cakes" are stuffed with dates or other tasty sweetmeats, and parcels of warka pastry with delicious fillings take a myriad of shapes. Some are long and thin like cigarettes. *Briouats* ("BREE-oo-at") are triangular and are dipped in simmering honey. Special favorites are the crescent-shaped "gazelle's horn" pastries and the flat, baked rounds of "coiled serpent" cake. Both are stuffed with flavored almond paste and dusted with confectioners' sugar. No less sweet and tempting is *ktaif* ("ke-TIE-ff") with its sheets of butter-fried pastry spread with a mixture of almonds, cinnamon, and confectioners' sugar moistened with orange-flower water.

Some of the many varieties of Moroccan pastries.

In the days when spices and essences were expensive items, these mouthwatering delights were only available to sultans, caliphs, and the like. Today sweet cakes are part and parcel of festive family occasions such as births and weddings and are also served on a day-to-day basis, when neighbors and and friends come together for a morning chat or afternoon break.

Sweet dishes, on the other hand, are special occasion dishes and are normally served before the fresh fruit or fruit salads with which an important Moroccan meal concludes. Sweet couscous garnished with prunes, raisins, and decorative trails of powdered cinnamon and confectioners' sugar, the sweet b'stilla concoctions, and a rice pudding studded with sautéed pine nuts and raisins steeped in orange-flower water fall into this category. All are sweet, rich, and celebratory and make a fine contrast to the fruit and nuts that follow.

IN ADDITION TO TEA

Although mint-flavored green tea is the main Moroccan drink, it is by no means the only one. In season every town has stalls piled high with mounds of golden oranges and tempting glasses of juice on display. Drinks based on citrus fruits, pomegranates, and grapes are very popular. So too are *sharbats*—fruit- or nut-flavored milk drinks with shaved ice— and sharp, yogurt-based thirst-quenchers. Morocco also has its own widely available mineral waters as well as numerous sodas.

Watersellers with elaborate dress and many cups are widely visible.

Café cassé ("ka-FAY KA-say")—half-and-half black coffee and hot milk— served in small cups is widely drunk. *Café Ras el Hanout* ("ka-FAY ras el ha-NOOT") is a spiced coffee. Ras el Hanout is a strong, ancient mixture of anywhere between 10 and 26 spices.

Wine is produced in vineyards first planted by the French, but most goes for export because devout Muslims do not drink alcohol.

EATING IN AND EATING OUT

Food and meals play an enormously important role in Moroccan family life. Cooking is regarded as an art, and family occasions—births, circumcisions, marriages, name days, and other events—are opportunities for a celebratory *diffa*, a banquet that may be more or less extravagant.

Finally, to round off a banquet, there is, as always, freshly brewed mint tea.

Everyday meals are relatively simple. Again depending on circumstances, the main meal for an ordinary family on an ordinary day may be a simple tajine, with meat if finances allow, or a dish of couscous with vegetables and meat if available. Alternatively there could be a nourishing, thick soup. Either way, the main dish is served with large wedges of bread, possibly with fresh fruit to finish, but almost certainly with hot mint tea.

Traditionally, meals are served on low, usually round tables. Diners sit on cushions around the table and use the thumb and first two fingers of their right hands to serve themselves from a central dish. Occasionally a spoon is provided, but bread is by far the most widely used implement.

Food stalls provide tasty snacks: bowls of steaming soup, hot chickpeas or broad beans, hard-boiled eggs dusted with cumin, meat grilled on skewers, simple salads, and sweet cakes. Freshly cooked ring doughnuts are threaded on string and carried home.

Dates for sale in a market.

BEEF TAJINE WITH ALMONDS AND PRUNES

3 lb.(1.5 kg) beef
2 tablespoons olive oil
1 teaspoon salt
$^1/_2$ teaspoon ground black pepper
1 teaspoon powdered cinnamon
$^1/_4$ teaspoon powdered ginger
$^1/_2$ teaspoon powdered saffron
3 short cinnamon sticks

4 oz. butter
2 large onions
$^1/_4$ cup (60 g) sugar
1 strip lemon peel
1 lb. (480 g) dried prunes
blanched almonds
fresh watercress or mint

Combine the oil and ground spices in a bowl. Cut the beef into cubes, chop the onion finely, and mix both into the oil and spices. Let stand. Sear the meat lightly in the butter, add any remaining marinade and enough water to cover. Simmer until meat is tender. While the meat is cooking, cover the prunes with boiling water and leave to stand for 20 minutes. Drain the prunes and cook them in a small amount of liquid from the meat. Add the lemon peel, cinnamon sticks, and half the sugar. Stir the remaining sugar into the meat. Arrange the meat and prunes and their sauce on a serving dish. Boil the remaining liquid from the meat rapidly to reduce it by half. Pour over the meat and prunes. Garnish with almonds sautéed in a little butter and with watercress or mint. Serve with rice or couscous.

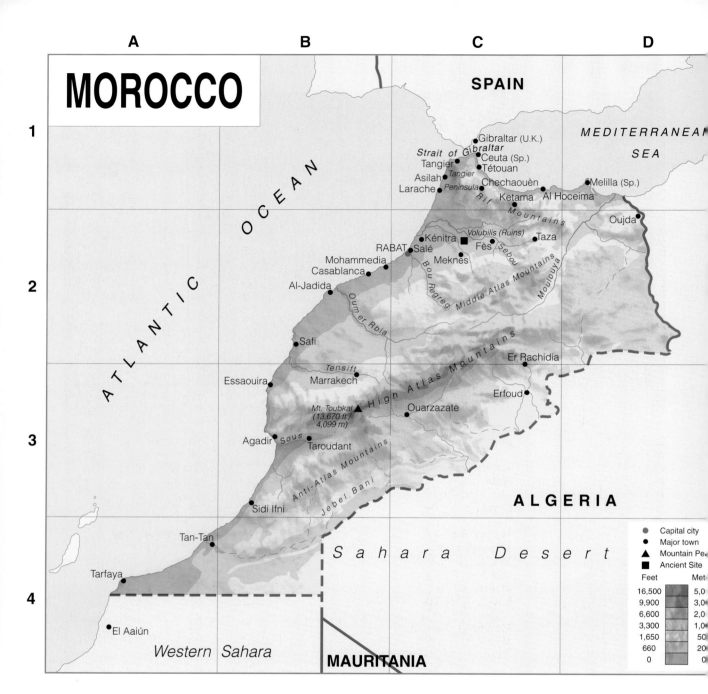

MOROCCO

A **B** **C** **D**

1

SPAIN

MEDITERRANEAN SEA

ATLANTIC OCEAN

Gibraltar (U.K.)
Gibraltar
Strait of Gibraltar
Tangier ● Ceuta (Sp.)
● Tétouan
Asilah ● *Tangier* Chechaouèn
Larache ● *Peninsula* ● Ketama ● Al Hoceima
Melilla (Sp.)

Rif Mountains

Oujda

Kénitra *Volubilis (Ruins)* Taza
RABAT ● Salé ■ Fès
Mohammedia ● Meknès *Sebou*
Casablanca ●
Al-Jadida ● *Bou Regreg* *Middle Atlas Mountains* *Moulouya*

2

Oum er Rbia

Safi ●

Tensift Er Rachidia ●
Essaouira ● Marrakech ●
High Atlas Mountains
Erfoud ●
Mt. Toubkal ▲ Ouarzazate ●
(13,670 ft / 4,099 m)

3

Agadir ● *Sous* *Anti-Atlas Mountains*
Taroudant ●

Jebel Bani

ALGERIA

Sidi Ifni ●

Tan-Tan ●

S a h a r a   D e s e r t

Tarfaya ●

4

● El Aaiún

Western Sahara

MAURITANIA

● Capital city
● Major town
▲ Mountain Pe[ak]
■ Ancient Site

Feet	Met[ers]
16,500	5,0[00]
9,900	3,0[00]
6,600	2,0[00]
3,300	1,0[00]
1,650	50[0]
660	20[0]
0	0

122

Agadir B3
Al Hoceima C1
Al-Jadida B2
Algeria C3
Anti-Atlas Mountains
   B3
Asilah C1
Atlantic Ocean A3

Bou Regreg R.   C2

Casablanca B2
Ceuta C1
Chechaouèn C1

El Aaiún A4
Er Rachidia C2
Erfoud C3
Essaouira B3

Fès C2

Gibraltar C1

High Atlas Mountains
   B3

Jebel Bani B3

Kénitra C2
Ketama C1

Larache C1

Marrakech B3
Mauritania B4
Mediterranean Sea D1
Meknes C2
Melilla D1
Middle Atlas Mountains
   C2
Mohammedia B2
Moulouya R. C2
Mount Toubkal B3

Oujda D2
Oum er Rbia R. B2
Ouarzazate C3

Rabat B2
Rif Mountains C1

Safi B2

Sahara Desert B4
Salé C2
Sebou R. C2
Sidi Ifni B3
Sous R. B3
Spain C1
Strait of Gibraltar C1

Tangier C1
Tangier Peninsula C1
Tan-Tan A4
Tarfaya A4

Taroudant B3
Taza C2
Tensift R. B3
Tétouan C1

Volubilis C2

Western Sahara A4

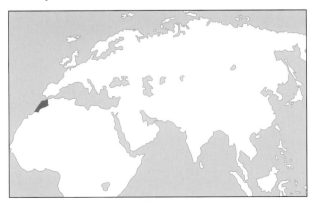

QUICK NOTES

OFFICIAL NAME
Kingdom of Morocco

HEAD OF STATE
The monarch, currently King Hassan II

AREA
177,117 square miles (460,504 sq km); 274,461 square miles (710,850 sq km) including the disputed Western Sahara

POPULATION
24,487,000 (1991 official estimate; includes Western Sahara, with a population of 163,868 in 1982)

CAPITAL
Rabat

COMMERCIAL CAPITAL
Casablanca

MAIN TOWNS
In order of size: Casablanca, Marrakech, Rabat-Salé, Fès, Oujda, Kénitra. (Continuous migration the countryside to the towns means that figures and order quickly become out of date.)

MEASURES
Metric system

TIME
Rabat is five standard time zones ahead of Eastern Standard Time

HIGHEST POINT
Mount Toubkal, 13,670 feet (4,101 m).

LANGUAGES
Arabic (official); French widely used in administration, commerce, and industry; three Berber dialects

RELIGIONS
Islam

CURRENCY
Moroccan *dirham*, which is subdivided into 100 *centimes*

MAIN EXPORTS
Clothing, phosphates and phosphoric acid, shellfish, fertilizers, hosiery, citrus fruits and other agricultural produce, canned fish

MAIN IMPORTS
Crude oil, wheat and other foods, machinery and chemicals

IMPORTANT ANNIVERSARIES
Independence Day, January 11
Feast of the Throne Day, March 3
Green March Remembrance Day, November 6

MAJOR RELIGIOUS FESTIVALS
Muslim New Year, *Muharram* 1
Aïd es Seghir (at the end of Ramadan)
Aïd el Kebir
Mouloud (birthday of the Prophet Mohammed)

GLOSSARY

Aïd el Kebir ("ah-EED el-kay-BEER")
Muslim festival commemorating Abraham's willingness to sacrifice Isaac.

Aïd es Seghir ("ah-EED es-say-GEER")
Muslim celebration marking the end of Ramadan.

djellaba ("jeh-LAH-bah")
Traditional long outer garment, usually with a hood and worn by both sexes.

fantasia
A display of horsemanship, traditionally part of a moussem.

hammam ("HAHM-mahm")
Turkish-style public bath.

imam ("ee-MAM")
Person who presides over the prayers in Islam.

imdyazn ("IM-dee-AZN")
Professional musicians who traveled from village to village singing the news.

Insha'Allah ("in-SHAH-lah")
Expression meaning "God willing."

kaftan
Moroccan woman's traditional long dress.

kasbah ("KAHS-bah")
A chief's residence, a fortified house, or an entire fortified village.

kif
Hashish, marijuana.

El Maghreb el-Aqsa
Morocco's Arabic name, meaning "the farthest west."

marabout ("MAH-rah-boo")
Saint or holy person.

medersa ("may-DER-sah")
Religious boarding school or students' lodging house.

medina ("may-DEE-nah")
Old, medieval part of a city or town, as distinct from the French "new town."

moussem ("MOO-sem")
Local festival in honor of a marabout.

muezzin ("MWE-zin")
One who calls the faithful to prayer, usually from the minaret of a mosque.

Ramadan
Muslim month of fasting.

Salaam oualeikum ("sa-LAAM wa-LAY-koom")
A Muslim greeting meaning "Peace be with you."

souk ("sook")
A stall in a market, or a whole market of stalls.

BIBLIOGRAPHY

Bowles, Paul. *Morocco*. New York: Harry N. Abrams, 1993.

Gumley, Frances. *The Pillars of Islam: An Introduction to the Islamic Faith*. London: BBC Books, 1990.

Lerner Publications. *Morocco—In Pictures*. Minneapolis: Lerner Publications, 1989.

Mernissi, Fatima. *Doing Daily Battle: Interviews with Moroccan Women*. Rutgers, N.J.: Rutgers University Press, 1989.

Nelson, Harold D., ed. *Morocco, A Country Study*. Washington, D.C.: U.S. Government Printing Office, 1986.

Wilkins, Frances. *Morocco*. New York: Chelsea House, 1988.

INDEX

INDEX

INDEX

PICTURE CREDITS

Christine Osborne: 10, 12, 15, 36, 39,
   42, 47, 49, 57, 60, 64, 67, 68, 70,
   73, 75, 81, 90, 99, 104, 114
HBL Network: 3, 4, 5, 6, 7, 8, 11, 13,
   20, 23, 25, 26, 30, 31, 37, 40, 43,
   46, 48, 51, 52, 55, 56, 58, 59, 66,
   72, 74, 76, 77, 78, 79, 82, 84, 87,
   88, 91, 92, 94, 106, 110, 111, 113,
   115, 119, 120, 121
Hulton Deutsch: 27
Hutchison Library: 19, 21, 24, 28, 32,
   54, 109
International Photobank: title page, 14,
   41, 44, 98
Pat Seward: 16, 18, 29, 34, 38, 45, 50,
   53, 61, 62, 63, 69, 80, 86, 89, 93,
   95, 97, 100, 101, 102, 108, 112, 118
Richard I'Anson: 71, 96, 103, 116